I0472710

PARABLE

POINT

PRESENTATIONS

The Most Effective System
For **Winning More Clients**
In The Complex Sale

Pelè Raymond Ugboajah, PhD

The intuitive mind is a sacred gift, and the rational mind is a faithful servant. We have created a society that honors the servant and has forgotten the gift.

- ALBERT EINSTEIN

For my family.

CONTENTS

PARABLE POINT PRESENTATIONS

The Most Effective System
For **Winning More Clients**
In The Complex Sale

The Three Big Mistakes

"I think that we as a people have become unaccustomed to having real conversations with each other, where we actually give and take to arrive at a new answer. We present to each other, instead of discussing."

- CATHLEEN BELLEVILLE
Former Microsoft PowerPoint Product Planner, 1989-1995

In 2002, a prominent sales executive in a fortune 500 company received a letter from a prospective client after delivering what he thought had been a very detailed, informative, and persuasive presentation. Let's call him Dave. In Dave's mind, this letter was probably just a formality – a kind word or a quick thank you note for his excellent work on the client's account. He had already started counting the dollar signs on the fat, six-figure commission check he expected to receive from this sale. During the course of a six-month campaign, he had built so many great relationships at this organization that he was sure that his recent presentation to their decision-making team had simply clenched what was sure to be a done deal. He pictured himself lounging on a beach with dark glasses and a Piña Colada in Cancun, or the Bahamas, or maybe even in Jamaica. Snapping out of his daydream, he carefully opened the letter and discovered the most shocking memo he had seen in years:

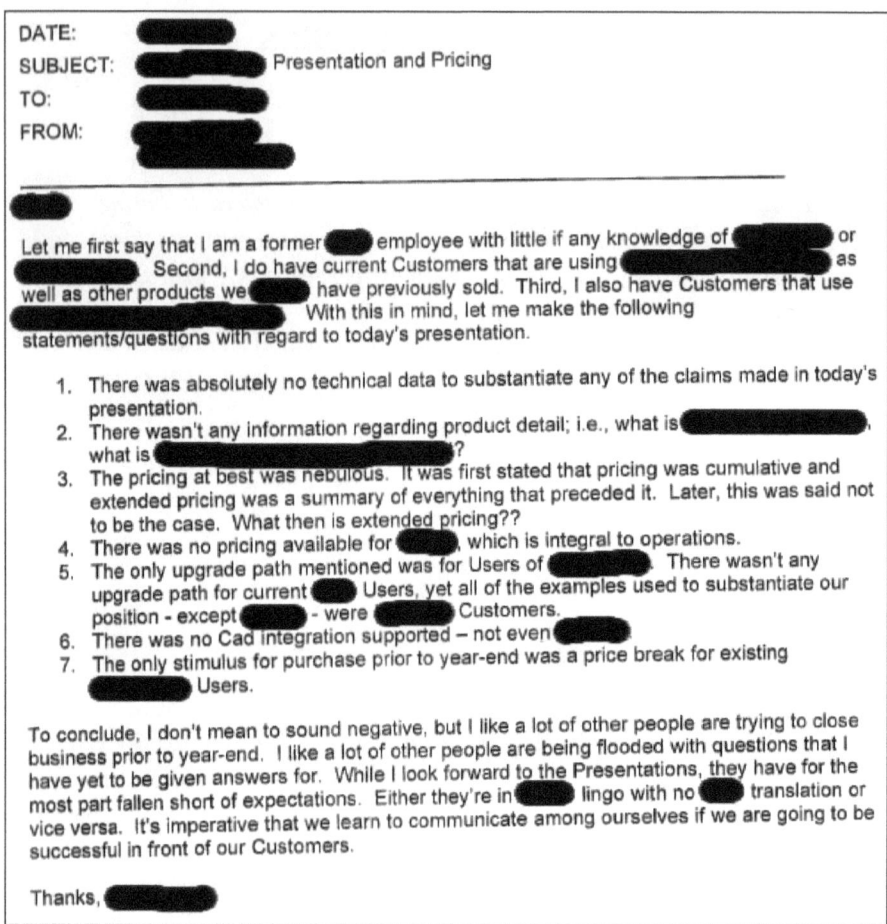

Figure 0.1. A Prospective Client's Memo to Dave (All identities protected)

The memo you've just read vividly illustrates the regretful, one-way communication in today's business-to-business presentations. It also shows how many of us find it difficult to accurately rate the effectiveness of our own presentations. Look at the following statistic about how most executives rate their presentations:

"**86%** of executives/managers rate themselves as effective communicators. Only **17%** of their audiences agreed."
                                        - (Clarke & Crossland, 2002)

If it's true that most of us think we're great presenters, then it makes perfect sense why Dave would think he gave a brilliant presentation when in fact he didn't. It is also easy to see why many people don't spend the time or follow a system for carefully practicing and perfecting their presentations – and why they assume that they can just *wing it* when it comes to presenting. Above all, this client memo demonstrates the ineffectiveness of most bullet-point, data-overloaded customer presentations today. In total, we are left with the crucial question: "How can we do a better job of interactively conveying business points and influencing prospective clients – without losing them in a sea of jargon?"

Whether you are a corporate sales executive or an independent service professional, your ability to grow your business is determined where the rubber meets the road – in the business presentation boardroom. Multiple studies have demonstrated the ineffectiveness of bullet-point, data-heavy business presentations, yet people keep depending on them, in part because they seem to have become a convenient mitigation for the widespread fear of public speaking. People are relying more on their software presentation tools and conversing less with clients, which begs the question: "How do you win more clients during business presentations, especially when you're not effectively interacting and communicating with them?"

> The complex, business-to-business (B2B) sale involves several relationship-building stages, but none is as mission-critical as the formal business presentation, especially when your products are technical or intangible in nature. The client's **perception** of your product's value after a meeting can easily be the difference between success and failure in long, expensive sales campaigns. This book is about how to turn those presentations into critical assets that will help you **win more clients** and shrink your sales cycles.

Indisputably, business professionals in every category struggle to communicate the value of their products to prospective clients. Consider this: over a million businesses are started annually in the United States, yet 50% – 80% of them will close in the first five years (Headd, 2003; Gerber, 1995). In a testimony to the United States Senate, Dun & Bradstreet revealed that 70% of these failures are because of competitive weakness and inadequate sales (Edmunds, 1979). One could easily infer that many professionals are neither persuading enough clients, nor adequately communicating the value of their offerings in sales interactions. As a result, many ventures are paying the ultimate price: extinction.

The problem this book addresses is the sad fact that an alarming number of B2B sales and service professionals really *struggle* with delivering effective business presentations that win clients – and I mean that kindly. Even though they are experts in their product's features and benefits, they struggle with bridging their clients' "value perception gap" – a situation whereby their prospective clients are not clearly convinced of the value of their offerings. The result of this value perception gap is long, expensive sales cycles, and most important, a dismally low client conversion rate.

This book is the result of a simple research question: "What is the most **effective** way for a professional to win more clients in the complex sale?" I placed this question at the center of my doctoral dissertation research, determined to find an answer that was empirical and supported by **science**, as opposed to mere opinion or conjecture. This book is the result of that scholarly exploration, coupled with years of experience giving winning presentations to diverse business audiences.

An important distinction: an *effective* business presentation is not measured by whether or not people enjoyed it, laughed during it, or felt warm and fuzzy at the end. Certainly, those audience reactions are nice, but a truly effective, *influential* business presentation is determined by how many people were persuaded to buy something or take action toward a buying decision after it is over.

Have you ever attended a mission-critical presentation in which you kept looking at your watch to see when it would end? Have you ever found yourself nodding off to sleep in the middle of an important, but painfully boring business speech? Most important, have you ever wondered why you didn't want to take any action at the end of a detailed, information-rich presentation, even though the presenter, smiling eagerly, admonished you to buy the product *now*? If you have ever wondered about, or experienced these things, then you fully understand the 'problem with business presentations'.

According to an online Microsoft article:

> Microsoft estimates there are 450 million users of PowerPoint™ giving around 1 million presentations a day – the vast majority of which have a dark background and bullet-points with white text. This is more commonly known as death by PowerPoint" (Microsoft, 2006).

With numbers like these, can you imagine the enormous travel and logistical expenses, bottom line losses, and absolute waste of organizational time and resources that ineffective business presentations can cause? Even Microsoft calls it *death* by PowerPoint – referring to the deplorable way most people use their software! On the flip side, imagine the potential for amazing benefits that can be gained when business presentations get to the point and *inspire* clients to action! Your organization will be leaner, more effective, and your business presentations will turn into a core competitive advantage, not a liability or a chore. You'll be greatly rewarded when your clients leave your presentations as *disciples*, and go to work for you, helping you reduce your sales cycles and increase your conversion rates. If a core aspect of your business involves giving presentations that must win clients, then you *must* read this book.

THE 3 BIG PRESENTATION MISTAKES

Based on over ten years of sales experience and a three-year doctoral dissertation exploration, I have found that there are essentially three big presentation mistakes that most sellers make, which result in lower client conversion rates, wasted organizational resources, and longer, more expensive sales cycles. In the complex sale, business presentations really shouldn't be a struggle if you can correct these three mistakes and approach them from the right mindset and strategies.

As we discussed earlier, many sellers struggle because their presentations are not really *conversations* – they are more like one-way, bullet-point reports. Beyond being expected to listen, clients are rarely involved in the presentation process. With this approach, how then can one be surprised if a client receives absolutely no value in exchange for the time spent listening to a presentation? For example, most of us would like our clients to respond with the following words after an important meeting:

"Aha! Now I get it!"
"Can you come back and share more of this with … '"
 "When can we get started?"

However, we know that this is not usually the case. Far too many sellers who have not mastered the critical sales presentation process hear their prospective clients say things like:

"Thanks! It's really crazy around here, but we'll be in touch."
"We probably need to think about it some more."
"Your product seems really interesting, but it's probably not for us."

Clients cannot and should never be held responsible for these kinds of responses, or for being completely uninterested in a seller's presentation. It is up to you, the seller, to make the appropriate connections with clients. The response you get from clients is the best arbiter of your presentation's effectiveness. In the end, the reason why most B2B sales professionals struggle with presentations is because they tend to make three big mistakes that preclude them from winning as many clients as they want and deserve. Here are the three biggest presentation mistakes that professionals make in the complex sale:

1. They inadvertently display a **'ME'** mindset throughout their presentations, and don't connect emotionally with clients.

2. They rely too much on **PowerPoint**™, almost as a crutch to mitigate the fear of public speaking. As a result, presentations are usually one-way bullet-point lectures, as opposed to meaningful, **diagnostic** conversations.

3. They don't have a clear **system** for preparing, perfecting, or continuously improving their business presentations, despite the fact that **90%** of their working time is spent **communicating** in high-value sales activities.

Fortunately, there is a better way, and it's built around the age-old, yet scientifically verified practice of influential business storytelling. You can learn how to win more clients through business presentations, and in fact, you can turn the medium into a competitive advantage for all those who interact with clients in your organization. The presentation phase of your complex B2B sales cycle can be just as rewarding as every other business activity you perform. You'll become much more enthusiastic about the format when you start to see prospects turn into clients as a result of your new approach.

WHY THIS BOOK WAS WRITTEN – AND FOR WHOM

This book is about *winning more clients* in the complex sale – and the way to do that is by overcoming the three biggest presentation mistakes that most sellers make. The focus of this book is therefore on how to achieve greater influence with clients in business presentations. There are many other resources that can teach you the technical aspects of how to speak with confidence, how to handle the fear of public speaking, how to create better PowerPoint slides, how to use audio-visual equipment, and so on. This book intentionally does not address those technical issues in great detail because they have very little to do with the science of influence, or with what inspires clients to action. If anything, many technically excellent presentations are the most boring of all, and convince absolutely no one to take action. Technical proficiency falls under the category of what you do to perfect your delivery *after* you know how to think about the art and science of persuasion. It is critical that you first understand how to think about business presentations, before jumping into what you must do to polish and perfect them. Beyond just being a *how-to* book on business presentations, this book presents a repeatable, duplicable system that shows you *how-to-think* about the ancient art and more current neuroscience of persuasion. Once you know how to think about influence, how to *do* it will come much more easily, naturally, and predictably.

> A **parable point presentation** is a template-driven approach to creating, delivering, and measuring client-winning business presentations.

This book was written for business-to-business (B2B) professionals who sell complex or intangible products and services. Examples of these professionals are:

- Sales managers
- Sales, presales, and marketing executives
- Independent service professionals

At LeaderPractice, the clients we serve are typically leaders in B2B organizations that deliver mission-critical presentations to multiple decision-makers and diverse audiences. These professionals are experts in their products and services, but frequently face the challenging *value perception gap* between their products' true value, and the value perceived by prospective customers after business presentations.

THE VALUE PERCEPTION GAP

A value perception gap occurs when your clients do not perceive the same value in your products as you do – or when they simply don't perceive enough value in order to make a buying decision in your favor. How many products do we see on the market that we feel are sub par in quality, and yet, people keep buying them while superior products languish? Far too many! Clearly, people buy things based on their own perceptions of truth, not necessarily on any absolute, finite truth that may exist. If clients could read minds, then they might instantly perceive your product's value with little or no effort. But alas – this is not the case. Your number one job as a business presenter is to manage audience perceptions.

Here is an example of how a perception gap can occur. Imagine if a client asked each member of your sales team the following questions. What would they say?

- How does your solution solve our problems?
- What results can we expect if we implement your solution?
- Why is your company different or better than the competition?

Would all of their responses be appropriately customized to meet the needs of that specific client, while remaining on-target with your corporate message? The gap occurs when your sales force struggles to manage the perceptions of prospective clients, and each individual sales person ends up doing it differently in their presentations – some with better results than others.

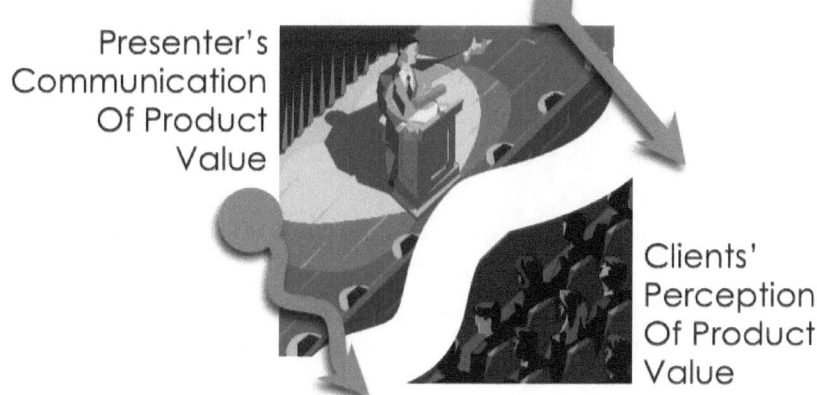

Figure 0.2. The Value Perception Gap

If you have this challenge, then you are not alone. Companies routinely spend millions of dollars on advertising and marketing campaigns, whereas their greatest client-facing assets – the salespeople – are left to their own devices at presentation time! According to research conducted by the American Marketing Association, Booz Allen Hamilton, and the CMO Council:

- Salespeople spend 40% of their time creating customer-facing presentations, while leveraging less than 50% of the materials created by Marketing.
- Only 10-20% of salespeople are creating compelling content that is consistent with corporate messaging.

- 85% of a companies brand and client purchase decisions are determined by the direct interaction of the "feet on the street" - the sales force interacting with their target buyers.

If you want to increase your client conversion rate company-wide, you need a business presentation solution that empowers your entire sales force, allowing them to be more effective in their inevitable customization activities.

If any of the following apply to you, then you should read this book:

- You sell or market technical or intangible subject matter.
- You would like to see an increase in client conversion rates.
- You would like to reduce sales cycle times and costs.
- You would like to differentiate yourself sharply from the competition.
- You would like to connect better with your audiences, get to the point quickly, and inspire them to action.
- Your sales team spends a great deal of time customizing your marketing department's presentations to suit their specific customers.
- You would like to implement a powerful, company-wide messaging and delivery system that will help your team *win more clients* with compelling content that is both persuasive to customers, and consistent with your core corporate messages.

IF YOU WANT TO CATCH A FISH, THINK LIKE ONE

At this point, you might be thinking:

"If it's so easy, why hasn't everyone already solved this problem? Why do I need parable point presentations?"

First of all, presentations are *not* so easy! The reason people haven't solved the 'business presentation problem' is that its roots are deeply ingrained in the way we think, act, and perceive the world. This is why a new mindset and paradigm shift are needed. Much of the literature on this subject recommends tactics and quick-fix actions, without dealing holistically with the core mindset and science behind influence in presentations. For example, as you'll learn in chapter six, (Your Biggest Presentation Challenge – is You), many professionals see the world from a *ME* perspective, and don't even realize that this viewpoint shows up in every single word they utter, and in every single bullet-point slide they present. As a result, they approach business presentations from the wrong vantage point, and forfeit the opportunity for truly consulting and connecting with prospective clients. Simply learning a new tactic for presenting more one-way bullet-points is like trying to get somewhere on time by driving faster in the wrong direction.

What you need is to understand how your prospective clients' brains are working during your presentation. Here's the paradigm shift: if you want to influence your audience, you need to learn to *think* like them, and then create and deliver your presentations accordingly! You may have heard Lao Tzu's ancient proverb:

"**Give** a man a fish, and you'll feed him for a day. **Teach** him how to fish and you'll feed him for a lifetime."

With the parable point presentation system, we teach him **how to think like a fish**, so he can catch enough to feed himself and his village for generations to come!"

Most of today's presentation training literature deals with improving the tactics and strategies of the presenter without clearly aligning those strategies with what audiences really need. You have probably heard this nonsensical but popular presentation myth:

> "Tell 'em what you're gonna tell 'em ... then tell 'em, and then tell 'em what you just told 'em ... and then ask for the sale ..."

With all this telling going on, when do clients ever get a chance to get a word in edgewise about *their* challenges? The parable point presentation system takes a markedly different approach because it deals comprehensively with the mindsets and needs of both presenters and listeners. As a presenter, you are encouraged not only to clarify the assumptions and paradigms from which you operate in presentations, but also to *think* like your audience, so that you can more correctly apply the science of *influence* – the critical component required for winning more clients.

Another reason why professionals haven't solved the 'presentation problem' is that they don't know how to convert their many facts, features, and benefits into an interactive experience that can exert influence on listeners. The parable point presentation system is built around the age-old art of interactive storytelling – and storytelling is the most influential form of communication known to humankind! Parable point presentations will help you increase your ability to interactively converse with your clients and persuade them in business presentations – a skill set that will positively affect your career and financial bottom line.

Your goal is no longer to impress clients in one-way business presentations. It is to listen, learn, tell stories, and listen some more. At the end of it all, a transformation will occur in the minds of your listeners, and the decision they make in favor of your offering will be entirely their own! As the popular saying goes, the best sales people don't sell; they help customers buy. In this case, the most influential presenters don't present, they tell stories and listen.

THE 3 BIG SOLUTIONS

As we discussed earlier, there are three big mistakes that most sellers make. This book is organized around three big solution ideas that correct those mistakes, namely *BrainPath*, *QueryTalk*, and *ConversionTrack*. These three solutions are encapsulated in ready-to-use templates that will help you overcome the three biggest mistakes that most sellers make. If you understand and implement these solutions, you will become very effective at winning more clients in the complex sale. Ignoring these solutions will result in more of the same – ineffective, one-way bullet-point business presentations that leave audiences uninspired and unwilling to act in your favor.

The 3 Big Mistakes	The 3 Big Solutions
1. The **'ME'** Mindset	BrainPath™ Storyboarding
2. One-Way **bullet-point** slides	QueryTalk™ Storytelling
3. No **system** for improvement	ConversionTrack™

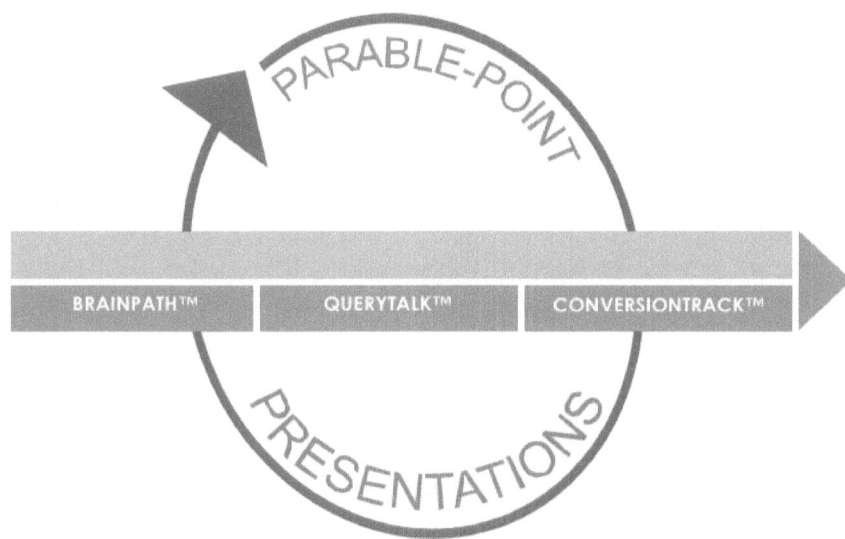

Figure 0.4. BrainPath, QueryTalk, and ConversionTrack

The preceding diagram shows the arrangement of these three solutions as the distinct parts of this book, and also defines the sequential learning process you'll follow to achieve your goal of winning more clients. Following this introduction, chapter one serves as a background that answers the question, "What is a Parable Point Presentation?" After this, we will examine the three main solutions in detail. These three solutions are represented in the diagram as an arrow that starts from today, and heads off into the near future, at which time you will have been transformed into a powerful, inspirational business presenter. Here now is a synopsis of the three main ideas in this book.

SOLUTION #1 – BRAINPATH

The greatest impediment to your success as an influential business presenter is not your public speaking ability – it is you – and your own mindset. In order to win more clients, you must orient your thinking away from a *ME* mindset, (i.e. your product's features and benefits), and think instead in terms of your *client's* point of view. There is a science behind the process of inspiring and influencing clients, and both of these desired effects are related to the way the human brain works – the *BrainPath*. The parable point presentation system is a cognitive approach to business presentations that is premised on the idea that you can only influence your audience if you understand what their brains need in order to reach a decision in your favor. By understanding *how* and *why* the human brain processes information and emotion, you will be better able to persuade others more consciously in presentations.

In SOLUTION 1: BRAINPATH, you will learn some of the most common business presentation myths, as well as the right mindset required for mastering the art and science of influence. You will gain a solid foundation for how to *think* about business presentations, which is a prerequisite for how to *do* them well. The last chapter in Part 1 is a hands-on, practical BrainPath™ template to help you create storyboards and content for your parable point presentations.

SOLUTION #2 – QUERYTALK

If you want to increase your influence in business presentations, you have to de-emphasize bullet-point slides, and instead, practice 'QueryTalk', which is a process of sharing stories and communicating via carefully planned Socratic questions throughout your presentation. The questions you ask will encourage your clients to share *their* stories and fully participate in becoming convinced about your solution. Natural, human protective mechanisms make it difficult for clients to believe all that you tell them, but if they say things themselves, then they will more readily become influenced. QueryTalk helps you get clients talking to you so they essentially help *sell themselves* on your solution during the presentation. You may have heard the old saying, "the best salespeople don't sell – they help clients buy!"

In SOLUTION 2: QUERYTALK, you will learn the biology of influence, the science of inspirational storytelling, and how to write and deliver business parables such as the critical parables of *Who, Why, and How*. At the end of Part 2 is a hands-on QueryTalk™ template for planning and designing your presentation delivery.

SOLUTION #3 – CONVERSIONTRACK

As we discussed earlier, most people have no clear system for practicing, perfecting, and improving their presentations. The fact is this: you can only improve what you can measure. The best system for practicing and improving your business presentations involves a process of continuous testing and measuring. What you have to do is spend time rehearsing in front of people, recording and videotaping yourself, and whenever you can, get written or verbal feedback from your client audiences. You also need to keep track of key performance indicators, such as client feedback and conversion rates, which will help you test, measure, and know what areas of your process to improve over time. Knowing where you stand is the first step toward reliably increasing your conversion rates and reducing costly sales cycles.

In SOLUTION 3: CONVERSIONTRACK, you will learn how to increase your client conversion rates through a systematic process of rehearsing, testing, and measuring your business presentations. At the end of Part 3 is a hands-on, parable point presentation 'PPP' Workbook, which will walk you through the process of creating, delivering, and measuring your parable point presentations.

> Over the past ten years, the parable point presentation approach has helped hundreds of professionals connect better, increase their influence, and convert more clients through business presentations.

As you begin this journey, please keep one thing in mind. This is neither a book of quick fixes, nor a bag of motivational tricks. If you are looking for a basic how-to book on overcoming the anxiety of public speaking, the parable point presentation system is not for you. This is a book about the right mindset and actions required for winning more clients during business presentations in the complex sale. Your goal is not about learning to convey more data, technical jargon, or better looking PowerPoint slides. Your goal is to learn to *think* like your prospective clients, reach more of their emotions, and as a result, inspire them to buy whatever you're selling. By reading this book, you'll soon have your audiences flowing down emotional rivers, reaching a sea of understanding, and not getting stuck in useless, muddy, data-filled embankments.

Ready? *Great*! Let's get started!

SOLUTION 1: BRAINPATH

The 3 Big Mistakes	The 3 Big Solutions
1. The **'ME'** Mindset	BrainPath™ Storyboarding
2. One-Way **bullet-point** slides	QueryTalk™ Storytelling
3. No **system** for improvement	ConversionTrack™

In order to win more clients, you must begin by examining your current beliefs and thought patterns regarding the business presentation medium itself. In Solution 1: BrainPath, you will gain new insights into how to use business presentations as a powerful client-conversion tool. You will learn that:

- You must move away from being a 'ME-focused', bullet-point, or benefit-point presenter, and become a 'CUSTOMER-focused', diagnostic, *parable point* business storyteller.

- You must shift to a *cognitive presentation mindset* in order to learn to win more clients with business presentations.

- Your *paradigms* – the way you see the world – are at the center of how influential your business presentations are.

- Any business presenter who hopes to influence clients must help them reach a mental state called '*Aha!*' – and the way to get there is by traveling along the *BrainPath* – the brain's evolutionary path of least resistance.

- The BrainPath™ template will help you organize and prioritize the best way to achieve trust, participation, and 'Aha!' from your audience

In solution 1, you will gain the crucial mindset and foundation that will prepare you for implementing the parable point presentation system.

1. What Kind Of Business Presenter Are You?

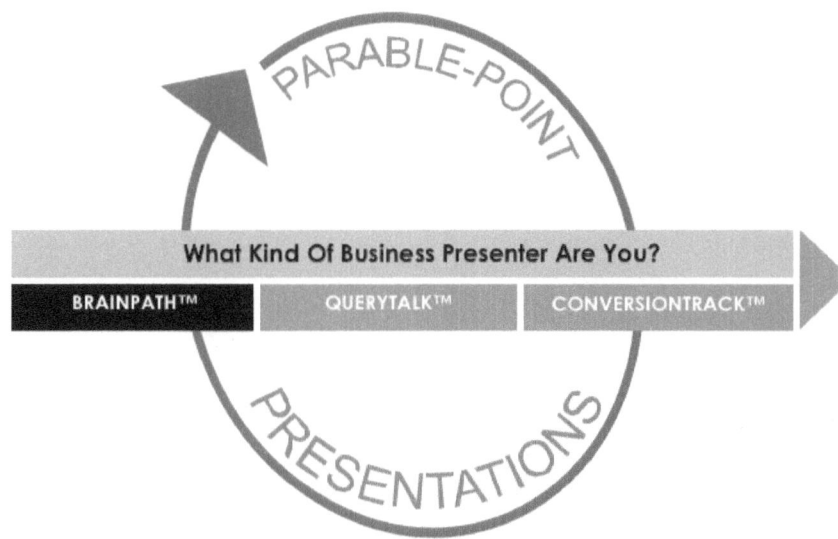

"Minds are like parachutes; they work best when open."
- LORD THOMAS DEWAR

D ata is sometimes the enemy of influence. Let me tell you a short story. It was three o'clock and we had now waited in our prospect's lobby for over an hour. After three airplane connections and a long wait, we were anxious for a chance to deliver our business presentation. Finally, one of our prospective client's employees ushered us upstairs to begin. However, she asked if we could give her a printed summary of our presentation because several of the expected attendees, including their CIO – the chief decision maker – were unable to attend. My technical sales director and I were devastated! We knew that the popular, data-rich business presentation where clients are 'bullet-pointed to death' had earned the format a bad name, but we were still astonished at how bad things had truly become. Even before our prospects had seen us, they had reached the conclusion that their very *attendance* was not a requirement – as long as they could get the bullet-points in handout form. They expected us to be bullet-point presenters, here to bore them silly with data-filled presentations like numerous other B2B solution providers had done before us.

In that moment, it occurred to me that the very notion of trying to 'present' more logic and data – especially in today's incredibly competitive, fast-paced, information age – was flawed. Any number of our competitors had probably already visited and presented their fact-laden bullet-points, claiming that they could satisfy all of the prospect's needs. There was simply no room for competitive differentiation by focusing on more of the same, and in a way, I could commiserate with our prospect for not showing up. *There had to be a better way!*

It dawned on me that winning this account called for true innovation! We needed to stop presenting, and instead, as a great teacher did some two thousand years ago, start telling stories – *parables* – that would make our points more powerful, and enroll our remaining listeners as 'disciples' of our cause. So, we did exactly that. We did not present bullet-points or demonstrate any technology that day. In lieu of my carefully prepared PowerPoint slides, I told three strategic parables that made points about how we could address their various challenges. I also asked lots of questions to get them to share *their* stories as well. The combination of telling and listening to stories was magical! By telling stories we bypassed their logical minds and connected with them; and by listening to their stories, we understood their challenges better and even helped them diagnose and clarify their unique needs. Eventually, all four of the attendees became evangelists of our organization's products and services as a result of the transformational, emotionally connected experience we created for them. They became the most valuable tool we had for spreading our message into their firm. When all was said and done, we won that complex sale by using parables – and made millions of dollars for our company – confirming for me the popular saying, *facts tell; but stories sell!*

THE THREE KINDS OF BUSINESS PRESENTERS

There are three kinds of business presentations, and they can be arranged graphically on a continuum of increasing effectiveness from 'bullet-points', to 'benefit points', to 'parable points'. It is important to start this journey by doing a quick, personal inventory of your current presentation tendencies. What kind of business presenter are you? In business presentations, do you *inform*, or do you *inspire*?

> "The mediocre teacher tells. The good teacher explains. The superior teacher demonstrates. The great teacher inspires."
> - William Arthur Ward

Figure 1.1 is the Business Presentation Continuum. It is based on an extensive scan of scholarly business literature I conducted as part of my PhD research, and from years of practical experience in complex sales environments:

	Least effective		*Most effective*
	BULLET-POINTS	**BENEFIT-POINTS**	**PARABLE-POINTS™**
Style	Unidirectional	Transactional	Cognitive
Effect	Inform	Persuade	Inspire
Approach	Features	Benefits	Diagnose Client Needs
Focus	'ME'	Product	Customer
Message	'Push'	'Push'	'Pull'

Figure 1.1. The Business Presentation Continuum

Many professionals are in the first category. They present with a lot of bullet-points, and the overall outcome is usually a one-way display of information. This communication style is *unidirectional*, characterized by a one-way push of information from presenter to listeners. These kinds of presenters usually start from their product's features, and try to make them relevant to listeners during the presentation. Not enough work is done to clearly communicate 'what's in it for the customer'. The result of this approach is an overly 'ME' or 'US' focused presentation that is low on emotional and persuasive power. Such presentations may inform, but they rarely influence listeners to action.

The second presentation category is the 'benefit points' method. This approach is an improvement on the first because it starts by asking what the benefits of a product or service might be to the customer. However, it is a *transactional* style, which means that it presents listeners with an unspoken exchange – "if you choose my product, I will reward you with the following benefits, such as a price discount and excellent, ongoing service programs." They promote the potential consequences, merits, or demerits of different client decisions, and rely on operant win/lose arguments to guide listeners to make a specific decision in their favor. Although this is still a product-centric, unidirectional 'push' of information, it is an approach that has a greater focus on benefits – for the client – and as a result, there is a much stronger potential for persuasion.

You might ask, "So, what's wrong with the benefit points approach?" Not much, upon first examination. In fact, this is much closer to what an effective business presentation should be: an experience that discusses the client's needs as much or more than the presenter's. Except for two things. First, the benefit points approach is characterized by an excessive use of bullet-point lists and minimal audience involvement. It is still a one-way lecture, not a conversation. Second, the benefit points approach is erroneously based on the assumption that you already know *exactly* what the client wants! Benefit point presenters believe that if they do enough prior research and show their audiences that they understand their needs – point for painful point – the performance will be more persuasive. Unfortunately, this approach rarely works in complex, mission-critical presentations. If you have ever sold a complex product, you are painfully aware that many customers, despite their best intentions, do not always know *exactly* what they want or need as a result of you simply presenting it, so you shouldn't assume too quickly that you do either. It is your job during the sales process and the business presentation to build a provider-client *diagnostic* relationship that will help clarify what the client really needs. This establishes a level of trust, and the client won't end up with a solution they don't need – which is in essence, a win/lose situation.

Here's an everyday example of this phenomenon. Imagine you felt ill and went to see a doctor. What if you arrived at the clinic, and the doctor immediately offered you an array of prescription drugs – 'solutions' – without first asking you a series of diagnostic questions? Would you consider that professional service?

Figure 1.2. The One-way, Bullet-point Approach to Presentations.

Probably not! That would be more like snake-oil salesmanship! A good doctor would probably ask you to share your *story* about what you feel and how you came to feel that way. She would then run a series of diagnostic tests on you before proclaiming what the problem is, and by extrapolation, what the solution might be.

In contrast to the bullet-point and benefit point approaches, the parable point presentation system is more diagnostic and customer-focused, and uses business storytelling to convey benefit points. It is a *cognitive*, interactive approach for producing emotional audience experiences. This means that the presentation features parables that are designed to conform to the way the human brain works, and are arranged in a manner that meets the least resistance in the minds of listeners. This process helps you *diagnose* the client's challenges during a business presentation – thereby resulting in a true win/win solution. By interactively exchanging stories and experiences with your listeners, you will be ensuring that your ultimate solution will meet their needs, inspire them, and will transform their business in a positive way. Your focus will be more on the 'CUSTOMER', and a solution that benefits all parties in the long run.

As the popular saying goes, you can lead a donkey to water, but you cannot make it drink. You cannot influence a client that is not actively involved in the business presentation process. However, you can help clients tell you what is most important to them – through their stories – so that you can point them towards solutions. As a professional, it is your responsibility to encourage your clients to share their stories, which will enable you to better assess their needs. This is also how to achieve lasting influence through business presentations: by inspiring, not cajoling:

transforming, not just transacting, and by doing so with storytelling and storylistening, not one-way bullet-point presentations.

> Wherever you are in the business presentation continuum, the goal of this book is to move you away from mere bullet-points, and closer to the shared storytelling and storylistening of the parable point presentation system. This will help you to connect with clients, more accurately diagnose their challenges, match their true needs with appropriate business solutions, and **inspire** them to action.

WHY BUSINESS STORYTELLING?

The business world has begun to understand and incorporate the power of storytelling into their arsenal of management tools. Leading companies like IBM and Coca-Cola now have dedicated business uses for corporate storytelling. Corporate storytelling consultants are leading the way to help companies realize that business narrative is more than a 'nice to have' skill, but is in fact a mission-critical organizational capability. The fact that good communication is required for leadership, sales, or any organizational endeavor is without dispute. Business narrative is becoming increasingly recognized as a powerful and influential form of communication in organizations.

An important distinction should be made between the growing field of organizational storytelling and the use of parable points in business presentations. The former is used for leadership, managing change, transferring vision, and increasing cooperation, while parable points are used to influence prospective clients in business presentations. Remember that a successful business presentation is one in which prospects are *converted* into clients, and the best way to do this is by systematically exchanging business stories. Consider this premise, which drove the research for a 1990s Fortune magazine article on selling:

Why are some people so good at selling, while others simply aren't?

To answer the question, the authors interviewed several top-performing sales professionals from a diverse cross-section of industries. Their research revealed two factors that were common to all of their survey participants:

1. They all sold without appearing like they were selling.
2. They all told stories.
   (Satterfield, 2006)

What these sales people practiced, and the key to converting more clients, is to exchange stories – a process that does not appear to be obvious selling, yet will open up your listener's minds and create a powerful emotional connection. Consider the words of Daniel Goleman, bestselling author of *Emotional Intelligence*:

> Insights made through stories do not alarm the psychic defenses. The rational mind does not quite perceive their challenge, and so does not resist. Thus these tales slip through the ego's defense, penetrating the mental prisons built by fixed habits of thought and perception. (Goleman, 1992, p. viii)

In today's ever changing, turbulent, highly competitive marketplace, converting clients requires more than fancy bullet-point presentations or sophisticated marketing campaigns. Frankly, your competitors have all become pretty fancy and sophisticated as well, and your prospects are dangerously close to considering you and your competitors to be commodity - 'all the same'. In this noisy, crowded information age, there is very little differentiation that you can create in a standard business presentation that cannot be quickly matched by your competitors. You have to go beyond one-way communication and *exchange* stories with your prospects. For example, the age-old claim that your product is faster, better and cheaper is no longer the ticket to winning customer attention and interest. Prospects have heard it all before, and your message is competing with the clutter of hundreds of rival messages in their minds at any given time. How can the business presentation – the moment of truth in all sales campaigns – be turned into a competitive advantage? How can sales, service professionals, and entrepreneurs who must continuously give business presentations improve their sales performance and client conversion rates?

The answer is this: **STOP** giving standard bullet-point presentations!

Yes, that's *exactly* what I am suggesting! Stop giving 'informational' presentations and start creating transformational customer *experiences*. To win more clients through business presentations, you need an entirely new paradigm – a new, holistic system of thinking – a totally different way of creating and delivering business presentations. Everyone has already been 'killed' by bullet-points, so why give them more of the same? It still takes several 'touches' to get a final sale, and some complex campaigns can run as long as eighteen months. All of this adds up to high sales acquisition costs, travel and logistics expenses, loss of efficiency, wasted time, and of course, wasted money.

The solution to this vast organizational challenge is found in your ability to *connect* with audiences through the well-known, ancient power of storytelling and storylistening. Here are some field-proven reasons why you should become a business storyteller and storylistener:

- Stories disarm.
- Stories are memorable.
- Stories are believable.
- Stories use *metaphor*, a powerful, indirect influence approach.
- Stories connect with people's emotions.
- Stories inspire!
- When clients tell you *their* stories, they drop their defenses even further, become more connected to you, and as a result, you can better diagnose their challenges.

By sharing and listening to stories, you create an interactive field in which you grow ever closer to your prospects' needs, and they in turn become more influenced by your points – both of which are factors that increase your likelihood of converting them into clients. You can certainly try connecting the old way, with one-way delivery of presentation bullets, graphics, and speech, authoritative rhetoric, or even motivational screaming; but the most effective method for connecting with clients happens to be based on the age-old, yet scientifically validated arts of storytelling, asking questions, and listening.

THE ANCIENT ART OF PARABLES

Long ago, in a land far away, there lived a man who was exceedingly wise. He was not materially wealthy, but his opulence in emotional wisdom was, and remains, unmatched throughout human history. One day, an apprentice approached him and asked a simple, yet poignant question: "Why do you speak to the people in parables?" The teacher looked at his protégé with wide, knowing eyes, and responded thusly, "This is why I speak in parables: Though seeing they do not hear, though hearing, they do not see" (Matthew 13:13, New International Version). It is important to note here that this man's message eventually became so successful, so inspirational, and so viral in its spread that it is still being repeated and followed diligently today, more than two thousand years later!

A **parable** is essentially a story – except that it is short, pithy, and communicates a powerful moral. A parable point is a business story with a mission; beyond being a narration of past events, it delivers a client **benefit point**.

In this book, the word parable is used interchangeably with the words story and narrative.

Jesus' response to his disciples foretold the *emotion-targeting* power of parables, and alludes to the scientific support behind their efficacy. We now know empirically that the human brain's signal path is wired in such a manner as to make sure that what we hear and see go through a preliminary gateway of emotions before we can fully process the stimuli we receive and turn them into actionable decisions (LeDoux, 1995). There is no evidence that Jesus was a dynamic public speaker, but he was certainly a master of using parables to connect and indirectly make powerful, memorable points. You will discover in chapter seven, (The Brain's Secret Path to 'Aha!'), just how intentional his use of parables were, and you will learn how to incorporate that power into your own presentations today. Jesus was a parable point presenter. Without the benefit of today's modern neuro-imaging systems, the man of Nazareth was right: if our emotions are not receptive, we will never truly be moved to action by what we hear or see.

WHAT IS THE PARABLE POINT PRESENTATION SYSTEM?

A business presentation should be viewed as a microcosm of an overall sales process. Far too many top sales people are excellent when it comes to relationship sales, but struggle in terms of *relationship presenting!* Parable point presentations, like any good relationship sales campaign, are built using an interactive *system* – where the whole is greater than the sum of the parts. In order to win more clients effectively and efficiently, you need to go beyond tactics, and implement a holistic system. Also, any system that is worth using must be based on proof – in this case, scientific research as well as practitioner experience.

Have you ever wondered why certain presenters are able to consistently make others laugh? Have you ever wondered why highly successful comedians like Eddie Murphy, Jay Leno, Chris Rock and others are able to hold your emotions in their hands and manipulate your funny bone with such ease and confidence? Well, here's how they do it: *they use a brain-based formula!* In a similar manner, the parable point presentation system is a field-proven, brain-based formula – but that is where the similarity ends. While a comedian wants you to laugh, a parable point business presenter wants the client to *think*, and wants to inspire them to action!

A parable point presentation is a three-point system, which is designed to correct the three biggest presentation mistakes that B2B sales professionals make. Let's recap what those are:

1. Displaying a 'ME' mindset and not connecting with clients emotionally.

2. Relying too much on one-way PowerPoint® slideshows, and not being diagnostic.

3. Having no clear system for preparing, improving and perfecting their business presentations.

Below are the parable point presentation system's core components and an explanation for each one of them.

1. **BrainPath**   (The mindset and process for creating Parables)
2. **QueryTalk**   (A diagnostic process for delivering Parables)
3. **ConversionTrack** (Improving, testing, and measuring Parables)

1. **BrainPath**: - You have to step away from the prevailing *ME* paradigm of creating presentations that exclusively reflect your product's features, benefits and business fit, and start focusing more on how your audience will actually *receive* your information. In essence, instead of just learning 'how to fish', you must learn how to 'think like a fish' in order to better anticipate their decision-making processes and engage them more successfully. BrainPath is a process of creating stories and parables that map to your customer's greatest challenges and are arranged for communication along the path of least resistance in their minds.

2. **QueryTalk**: - The predominant business presentation method today involves delivering one-way talks that don't adequately involve listeners. Studies have shown that you cannot fully influence people who aren't actively involved in the process. Once again, the paradigm shift is to understand that what you present really does not matter if your prospective clients don't get involved and ultimately take no action. You can make all the right benefit points, but if you get no audience reaction and interaction, there will be no effect on them. Unlike the snake-oil salesman approach, a parable point presentation is diagnostic, and provides ample opportunities for the clients' stories to be heard. *QueryTalk* is an interactive process of storytelling, asking Socratic questions, and listening, in order to fully engage audiences in the presentation process.

3. **ConversionTrack**: - In all other sales, marketing, or management activities, practitioners use key performance indicators to measure and track their progress. In sales, there is the forecast, which is measured against results. In management, there are goal and strategy statements that are measured against results. Yet in business presentations, most professionals simply go from one presentation to

the next, without learning any lessons from each experience or tracking their progress and effectiveness along the way. Testing and measuring results is what separates great business presenters from lucky, occasionally effective ones. *ConversionTrack* is a process of collecting and tracking feedback and conversion rate information from the prospective clients themselves. By testing and measuring the results of your business presentations, you are increasing your ability to improve them.

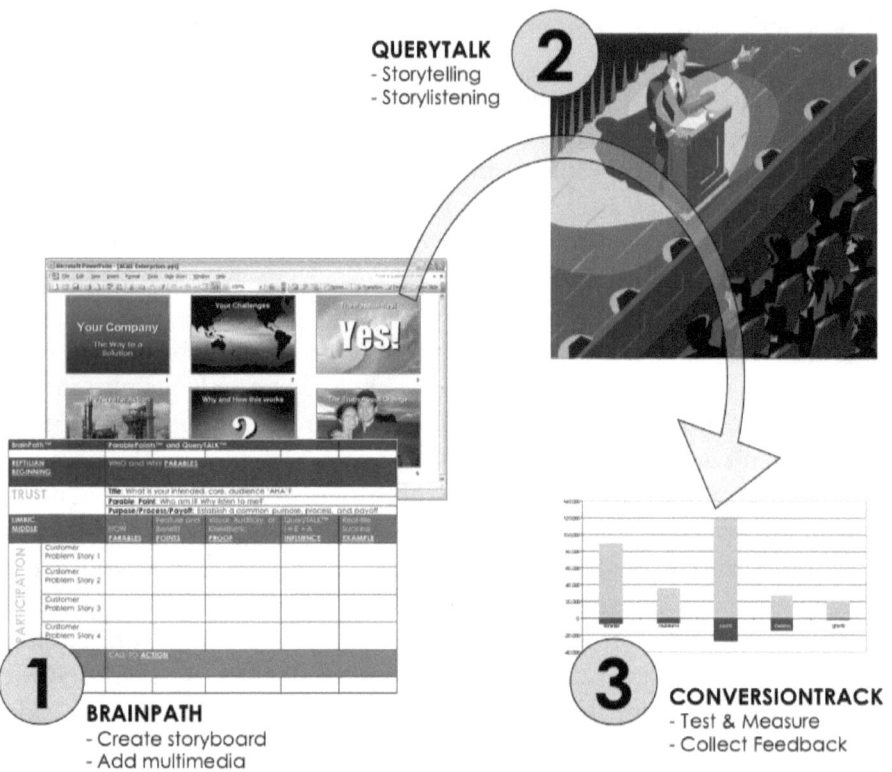

Figure: 1.3. The Parable Point Presentation System

The task of successfully winning more clients starts with an entirely new *mindset* for delivering business presentations. Instead of more of the same old bullet-point format, this three-point presentation system – creating, delivering, and measuring – will increase your ability to win more clients, whether or not you are comfortable with public speaking.

In addition to the system itself, you will learn how to write and create business parables that make powerful points. Throughout the parable point presentation system, as in any successful business presentation, you will need to tell stories – but not just any stories. You will need to deliver the *right* stories at the *right* time to make the *right* points. These stories are called parables points, and they are reusable short stories that explain what your audiences are most interested in: who you are, why they should listen to you, and how you can deliver value to them. Here are examples of the most powerful business parables you will learn to create and deliver as part of the parable point presentation system:

Parables of *Who*
- Who are you, and what do you do?
- Who are your listeners, and what are their needs?

Parables of *Why*
- Why should they listen to you, and what's in it for them?
- Why are you different from the competition?

Parables of *How*
- How do you uniquely solve their business challenges?
- How do your product's features truly benefit your listeners?
- How have other customers benefited from your solutions?

CAN ANYONE DO THIS?

Can anyone learn to create such emotional connections, you may ask? *Yes* – because we have *always* done so. Since the age of three years old, most of us have told stories that convey emotions. Without knowing it, you have been developing the skill of connecting emotionally through stories for years! Now all you need to do is hone that skill and target it towards your buying audience. Now you just need to understand, practice, and master the ancient art of speaking directly to people's emotions, not just their logical minds. Using stories to make points in business presentations is the pathway to creating emotional and persuasive connections. Storytelling is a powerful and learnable skill for bypassing people's doubting, cautious, logical minds, and entering into the place where true decisions are made – the biological realm of emotions.

The technology behind the skill of persuasive business presentations is found in the use of a particular kind of story – *business parables* – short, pithy allegories, which carry powerful metaphorical points that are difficult to forget. Instead of displaying slide after slide of tedious bullet-points, you will learn how to tell a series of powerful parable points! In today's Internet-speed concrete jungles, many ignore this timeless, mythical, primordial skill. Yet the ancient arts of storytelling and parable-making are still practiced in cultures all over the world. This book brings the ancient skill of inspirational storytelling into the boardroom, where parable becomes persuasion, a strategic business best practice, and a client-winning competitive advantage.

This book does not seek to promote any specific religious icon. A parable is simply a form of storytelling communication, and in this context, it has nothing to do with organized religion per se. However, Jesus' use of parables makes a very powerful proof point about the art of connecting emotionally and virally. He was practicing a form of persuasion over two thousand years ago that today's cutting-edge neuroscience now shows to be perfectly on target. The power of his presentations is still felt today, eons after he gave them, locked in the hearts and minds of millions worldwide. His marketing brand is still the most recognizable on earth, and it inspires such passionate action that people spend entire lives following his teachings. And yet, the majority of his teachings were through the secret power of parables! His formula, surprisingly simple and elegant, was to let the parables make his points for him; tell a parable, make a point; *tell a parable, make a point.*

Parables are among humankind's most influential, memorable, and viral tools for influence.

Despite all the changes the world has been through, not much has changed in the area of persuasive communication. The dramatic narrative, story, or parable is still at the center of how people become inspired. All of the world's greatest communicators - from Stone Age storytellers, to Euripides some 2,500 years ago, to present-day West

African griots – all have used storytelling and parables, which is not in itself a new invention. Why is it that parables, so innately and powerfully influential, are largely untapped in today's business world where persuasion is needed the most? How can you, regardless of your presentation skill-level, harness the power of parables to influence and inspire action in audiences today? The answer lies in your business presentation mindset – which is the subject of the following three chapters!

MY STORY: WHY I BELIEVE IN PARABLES

My introduction to parables began at an early age. As bombs and stray bullets flew over our heads in the middle of the Biafran war, my mother calmly told us short moon-time stories to uplift our spirits and shield our minds from the nagging pain of hunger. In my heart, *safety* was a moonlight story. This was my first opportunity to witness the power of emotion over logic. Somehow timeless stories, parables and proverbs lit up our hearts, strengthened our emotions, and blotted out the pain, hunger and despair that was all around us. Years after those miserable first beginnings, my mind has dulled out the details of war, but the feelings of safety and belonging that her parables created in me will last forever. My mother bypassed our minds, and connected to our hearts through the power of parables.

Later on in my life, I learned that the reason that my late father gave me the name Pelè – after the greatest soccer player on earth – was because of the influential power of a simple story. You see, in 1967, the Biafran civil war I mentioned above was brutal and raging ferociously, not unlike what has happened more recently in Rwanda, or Liberia, or Darfur. People were dying by the millions as tribes fought against each other in the young, post-colonial West African country. However, one day, a story began to spread from towns to villages. This story was so powerful, and was repeated so many times that it took on the power of a parable. The story everyone was talking about was that Pelè, the world's greatest soccer player, was going to come to the warring country for an exhibition match! (If you are familiar about how fanatical people can get about soccer, and Pelè, you'll know what I mean). This story became so powerful that when the time came for an official decision to be made, the leaders of the two warring sides, Biafra and Nigeria, came together and agreed to *stop* the war for 48 hours – just so everyone could come to the capital city of Lagos and watch Pelè play his exhibition match! Now THAT's influence! How many people do YOU know who can stop a war? When I thought about that event many years later, it occurred to me that no matter how much people loved soccer and Pelè, the real reason he was able to stop a war was because of the power of a story – repeated time and again until it took on mythical proportions, and until it reached the emotions of sworn enemies, softening their hearts, and bringing them to a better place on the negotiation table. My late father, a renowned PhD and business storyteller himself, gave me the name Pelè to celebrate the incredible, influential power of storytelling.

> Once again, my life's events were showing me that there is an intrinsic, emotional, **influential** connection that occurs when people hear stories and parables.

Despite these early introductions, I did not experience the full power of storytelling and parables until years later when I entered the corporate world. There, as a director of marketing at a global software corporation, I noticed a very strange thing. The number one practice in all of our work was putting together these extremely technical PowerPoint files and heading out to prospective client organizations where we would deliver the most tedious business presentations you could ever imagine. Like most of corporate America, we were PowerPoint warriors with no clue about the science of human influence. We simply traveled from city to city with our digital bundles of technical information, and delivered the same old tired messages that – almost without fail – would put audiences to sleep.

I soon realized that these meetings were so critical that their outcome could make or break million-dollar deals. On the one hand, a bad presentation could waste enormous organizational resources and kill an entire six-month sales and marketing campaign. On the other hand, a good one could keep us all in business. Amidst all this, I noticed an interesting trend. The naturally talented presenters connected with their audiences in a magical way, not too dissimilar from the effect I had experienced in Africa or in my grade school days, and that connection made the difference between a lost venture and a million dollar software deal. It was never really about the information they presented. In fact, some of them didn't even use PowerPoint slides. I soon noticed that those kinds of presentations had one thing in common. They involved short, pithy stories that left the audience emotionally engaged and *inspired!* I was reminded of Einstein's words, in which he opined that we live in a society that outwardly appreciates logic and reason, (the servant), over emotion and intuition (the master). Yet paradoxically, I could see that whenever it truly mattered, such as in critical business decisions, the master (emotions) always overcomes the servant (logic) in the mind of the decision maker. Therein began my love affair with the power of inspirational business presentations, and from that moment forward, I became a student of influence through storytelling.

One day, while selling our product at a very important client meeting in Texas, I decided to stop the cycle of drab PowerPoint presentations, and I decided to liven up the crowd a bit. The audience was still finding it difficult to understand and buy in to our software's concept of 'managing information anywhere, anytime, anyway'. So I did something very unusual. I turned off the PowerPoint projector and invited the entire audience to listen to a simple story. I proceeded to tell them a modern story – a 'parable of how' our software worked – and I concluded by explaining how unique requirements had brought our two companies together.

Here's the 'parable of how' I told them:

"On February 25, 1991, US-led forces entered Iraq and Kuwait with the goal of removing the Iraqis from Kuwait. One hundred hours later, they accomplished their objective. Norman Schwarzkopf, the American commanding general, described the engagement as having accomplished an overwhelming military victory with an amazingly low loss of life. One of the reasons why the allies were able to win so quickly with limited casualties was the technology they used.

Many of you will remember the Stealth fighter, Patriot missile system, and the M1A1 Tank. These were the visible pieces of the war, and we watched them perform every night on CNN. But the most significant advantage that US forces held was provided by something that couldn't even be seen – GPS global position systems. This was the first war where US commanders knew exactly where every physical asset was at all times. Commanders weren't forced to rely on sketchy reports or intelligence information. While the Stealth fighter, Patriot Missile system and M1A1 tank are all impressive pieces of technology, providing an infrastructure that would allow commanders to manage all of these assets was the key to our overwhelming success on the battlefield.

That's how our software works. The information you need is constantly being indexed in the background and made available to you in real-time, as though you have a global positioning satellite's view of your business information 'battlefield'. In order to win in today's competitive business environment, you need precise, visual, and immediate access to all your enterprise data – 'anywhere, anytime, and in any way.'"

I could see all the eyes in my audience light up immediately after that story. No one was asleep; they finally got it! The emotional and logical connections had been made; they got the parable, *and* the point. After that, I invited audience members to share their stories with the rest of us. When they spoke, we became the students, and they, the teachers. All of a sudden, we *connected!* A simple process of exchanging stories had excited them, disarmed them, and reached past their logical minds and into the hiding place of their emotions, where the final decisions would eventually be made. We won that deal, and even as I write this, I still have the company's plaque of appreciation hanging on my wall for my first multi-million-dollar deal. The success and money were great, but for me, the true significance of that occasion was my personal rediscovery of the power of parables.

After that pivotal experience, I continued to travel throughout the world as one of the company's first marketing evangelists, helping to turn its flagship product from a middleware software toolkit to a $200-million-dollar-a-year business in just under two years. Later, as the Director of Product Marketing at a $20-billion-dollar corporation, I continued to shake up audiences with my parable point approach. I began to read everything I could find on the impact of storytelling on people's emotions. I devoured every book I could find on the neuro-scientific underpinnings of the social phenomenon we call business presentations. This led me to eventually pursue a doctoral degree in business with a focus on the impact of storytelling and brain-based learning on organizational performance. I also joined Toastmasters, an internationally known public speaking organization, where I won several championships, all the way to becoming the International District Six Champion of Public Speaking.

I soon realized that it was my life's purpose to share this discovery with the world. I tirelessly researched the art and science of business presentations, and I discovered how current neuroscience was reinforcing my intuitive knowledge of the inspirational power of parables. It was also obvious to me that effective business presentations were not a trait-based affair, but rather, they could be learned and practiced by anyone who puts their mind to it.

The **parable point presentation system** helps you bypass the logical, doubting minds of an audience, so you can speak directly to their emotions, where science now reveals, a majority of their decisions are made.

The same technology and methods that I learned, built upon, and used to win speech awards and million-dollar deals are now made available to you in this book. Einstein was right: as a society, we've got it backwards. In truth, logic is but a servant; intuition and emotion are the genuine gifts we have at our disposal.

CASE STUDY

THE POWER OF STORYTELLING

In 1996, five people in a large, multinational organization of 15,000 had a radical idea for refocusing the core business. As a first step they brought together the 60 people they considered critical to their mission's success. The goal of the event: the group of five would become the de facto owners of the change initiative, garnering the support of everyone in attendance. The biggest obstacle: many of the 60 had competing, even hostile agendas – securing their unified support was daunting. After everyone had filed in, the emotional tension in the room was palpable.

Just after stating the topic at hand, each person was asked to tell the story of how he/she came to be in the room. Any kind of story would do, as long as it was true. People could play it safe and describe how they got up that morning and made it from their house to the Metro to work, or they could put some of their cards on the table, drawing the connection between their careers and the meeting's importance.

Within minutes there was a dramatic change in the atmosphere of the room. It became rambunctious and fun-filled as people took successive trips down memory lane. Others chimed in to add their two cents. By the time the exercise was over, just 30 minutes later, the tone of the room was transformed, from tension, quiet, and unease, to enthusiasm, laughter, and collaboration. The hard work was done.

Next, each person was asked to describe his/her ideal future for the organization. The details of these future-stories were captured on flip charts. At the meeting's conclusion, the group of five had established itself as the shepherds of the fledgling initiative.

Storytelling launched that meeting and continued to play a fundamental role in the change initiative. The effort made rapid progress in the next two years – from an unfunded idea to a worldwide program with $60 million in annual allocation.

(Kahan, 2006, p. 23)

CHAPTER 1 SUMMARY

WHAT KIND OF PRESENTER ARE YOU?

- This book is designed to help sales and service professionals convert more clients through business presentations.

- There are three kinds of presentations: bullet-points, benefit points, and parable points. Parable point presentations help you get past doubting, logical minds, and talk directly to people's emotions, thereby inspiring them to action.

- Stories are the most effective tool for influencing people. Parables are short, bite-sized stories that have the power to address the emotional mind in ways that logic and information cannot.

- Jesus is an excellent example of a parable point presenter, but any one of us can increase our persuasiveness in business presentations - if we learn a system for doing it.

- The parable point presentation system is based on three philosophies that drive its strategies:

  1. Present the way your client's think – along their **BrainPath**™
  2. Present through a process of **QueryTALK**™ – bidirectional conversations that allow both you and your clients to share stories.
  3. Test and measure the effectiveness of your business presentations through **ConversionTrack**™.

2. The Cognitive Presentation Mindset

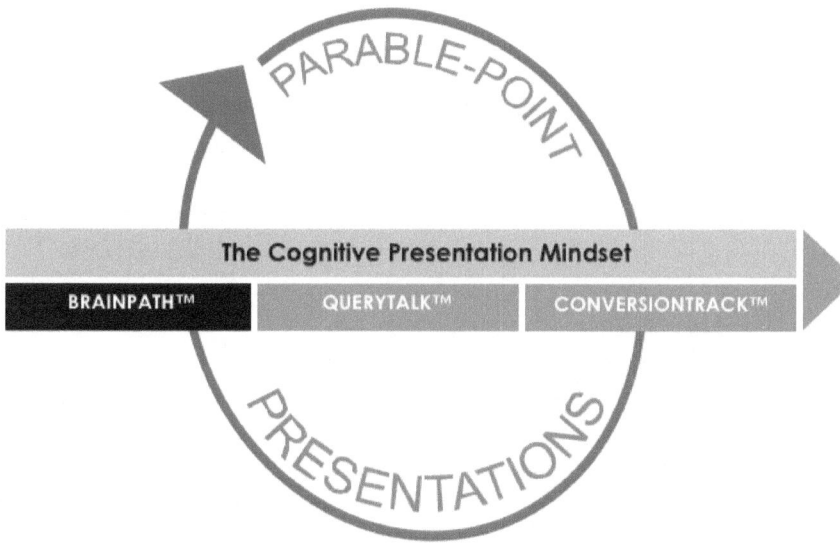

"We cannot solve problems by using the same kind of thinking we used when we created them."

- ALBERT EINSTEIN

What you are about to learn is completely contrary to what you've come to know as traditional, modern thinking. The popular mindset for conducting business presentations has always followed a specific, logical and predictable formula – 'first the problem, then the solution.' The reason we are so conditioned to this approach is because it is the predominant method for problem solving in the media, our culture, and our educational system. Yet unfortunately, (as most bored audiences can attest), this approach isn't working very well in business presentations. The business tools we use, such as PowerPoint, have only served to exacerbate the situation, and as a result, many of us have forgotten the very basics of the art of human influence. What we don't learn in our classrooms is that the outside world doesn't really follow the rules of order and logic that we find in textbooks. In fact, the real world is not an orderly place at all. It's a jungle out there, and the number one driver of problem solving in any jungle is emotion, *not* logic!

The reason you need to cultivate a certain mindset over another is premised on the idea that the way you think about something will determine what you do, which will of course determine the kinds of results you will get. If you want to change the results you're getting, there is no point talking about what to do differently, until you first talk about how to *think* differently. In chapter one we introduced the business presentation continuum, which showcased the three kinds of business presentation approaches that are possible, from the least effective bullet-points, to benefit points, and to the most effective method – parable points. We discussed the fact that most people present from the bullet-point approach, which according to most accounts, leads to bored audiences and dismal results. In the bullet-points approach, the business presentation platform is not optimally used for producing real influence – and is rarely treated as a core competitive advantage. To close deals, many people rely much more on their other relationship selling activities, while the business presentation is relegated to an almost incidental event. The purpose of this chapter is to help you change that way of thinking. You will learn actionable, new ways of thinking that will move you away from bullet-points, and towards parable points. I call this the *cognitive presentation mindset.*

THE COGNITIVE PRESENTATION MINDSET

Let's start with the popular order in which most people present information. First you present the problem, then you offer a solution, and then you discuss the various features and benefits of that solution. Seems logical, right? Well, the challenge is that even though it is logical, most people don't start off by responding to information logically. They respond *emotionally* first! What ends up happening is that presenters supply what may very well be the *right* information in the *wrong* order, resulting in clients that are bored out of their minds. Here's an example: how do you spell ART? "A. R. T.," right? Well, imagine if you used the same exact letters, but spelled them in a different order. You would get either RAT, or TAR – two words that have absolutely the wrong meaning, but the same letters. Today's popular presentation order is too focused on logic, and not enough on emotion. It is also premised more on the presenter's desire to deliver (sell) a solution, rather than on a listener's need to be emotionally stimulated in order to accept a solution. As such, most corporate B2B presentations start with, and are sometimes excessively long on the *about us* section, after which they jump right into the problem/solution format, without adequately connecting with listener's emotions.

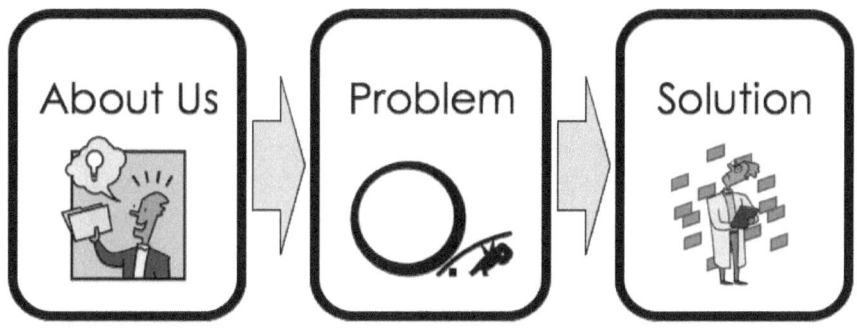

Figure 2.1. Today's Popular 'Problem/Solution' Presentation Mindset

The parable point presentation system encourages a completely different mindset for creating and delivering business presentations – the *cognitive* mindset. The cognitive mindset advocates a whole-brained approach to presentations, where not only logic, but also emotion is involved.

Figure 2.2. The Cognitive Mindset for Winning More Clients

Of tangential interest here is that western educational traditions are obsessed with the left-brained (logical, problem/solution) approach, whereas ancient, eastern, and African traditions are much more right-brained (emotional connection through storytelling). These two worldviews have merit because they have each evolved through human experience over the ages. The cognitive mindset gleans the best from both worldviews.

Imagine yourself as a speaker in front of a hundred people. Now close your eyes and imagine that all those people are really just *brains*, sitting on their brain stems while smiling and wagging their frontal lobes at you. If you were talking to brains instead of people, how would you act differently? You would probably feel prompted to speak in a language that brains can understand, right? That is the core principle behind the cognitive approach. This mindset views the task of business presenting as an exercise in which you are looking out into a room full of brains – not clients. Neuroscience tells us that behavior is based on how our brains process information. If the brain doesn't process the information in a certain manner, you won't get a favorable response, regardless of the truth of the data you are presenting. In other words, if you want to influence and win clients during business presentations, you must understand how their brains work, and build your presentation around that process.

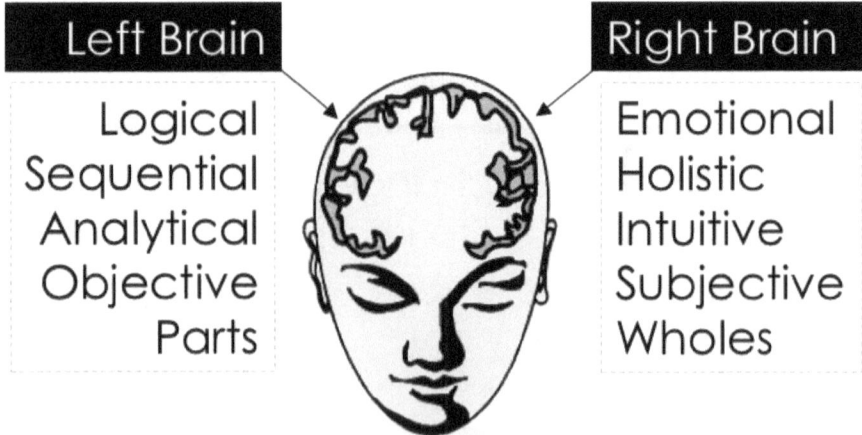

Figure 2.3. The cognitive mindset: presenting to a room full of brains

In the cognitive approach to presentations, the first order of business is to capture the audience's attention – without delay! You must get to the point – fast! This means you must quickly awaken people's conscious and subconscious *emotions*. In today's television and Internet generation, people have very little time to waste, and incredibly short attention spans. If you don't hit them hard and fast, you'll lose them in the first thirty seconds, and your entire presentation will become a tedious battle of 'catch-up'. There are many devices for capturing attention and simultaneously getting to your points fast; you could ask some poignant questions, tell a business parable, share some humor, or you could involve the audience in an exercise or a game. Whatever you do, the principle is this: people won't listen to you unless they are just as awake emotionally as they are physically.

The next step in a business presentation is to replace your bullet-points of features and benefits with *stories* about features and benefits. This is actually a bigger shift than it sounds. Research studies have shown that telling stories is much more influential than telling facts. Facts speak to the left brain, to logic; while stories speak to the right brain, to the emotions, which current research is revealing to have a greater influence on decision-making than people realize. The brain does not like to be assaulted and pushed too directly with data. Stories are a powerful, indirect way of making the same points, but with the added advantage of involving people's emotions. The more stories you can tell, and the more you encourage your clients to tell you *their* stories, the more they will understand and remember your product's features and benefit points.

The last, but most important thing you must do in a business presentation involves getting your listeners (their brains) to a place of '*Aha!*' – eureka! Scientists have shown that there is a surge of electrical activity that occurs in the right lobe of the brain when people experience insight, (also known as 'Aha!'). This excitable state usually leads to decisions that are in your favor, because now, the listener finally 'gets' your product's value – emotionally – and clearly understands how your solution delivers the benefits you promise.

An experiment conducted by professor Jung-Beeman et al. (2004) revealed that there are distinct brain mechanisms that lead to this breakthrough moment of 'Aha!' In the study, researchers compared subjects' brain activity in two different experiments. Participants were given a series of word problems to solve, half of which were intended to produce a distinct 'Aha!' moment, and the other half produced non-insightful solutions. Using brain-imaging devices, the researchers found that there was increased electrical activity in a small area of the right brain's temporal lobe right before the subjects reported experiencing creative 'insight' – otherwise known as 'Aha!' Comparatively, very little activity was found in that area during solutions that were not insightful.

This experiment is a great leap forward in our understanding of how the brain works. Scientists have known for a long time that the right brain is the center of emotions, but now we can deduce that by supplying the kind of stimulus that produces 'Aha!' we are increasing our chances of making that crucial emotional connection that leads to converting prospects into clients. The kind of stimulus needed is emotional, whether you do it through humor, or through a story that inspires strong feelings. It would be much harder for you to help people achieve this crucial state of insight by presenting data and logic alone, since logic registers on the left lobe of the brain. So, your goal as a business presenter is to provide a whole-brained experience, (logic *and* emotion), that will help your clients achieve 'Aha!' – that magical, excitable moment when they 'get it', *feel* how your solution solves their problems – and then choose your product or service.

CHANGING YOUR PRESENTATION MINDSET

The interesting thing about a mindset is that people aren't usually aware of it. Your mindset is hidden to you unless you examine it critically from another person's point of view. (You cannot see the picture when you are in the frame). For example, many people actually think they are good presenters, even though evidence is overwhelming to the contrary. Andy Goodman (2005), author of *Why Bad Presentations Happen to Good Causes*, conducted a survey to find out how presenters rate their own presentations – versus how good they thought other people's presentations were. Goodman's results were very telling:

Presentations I Give	Rated Good–Excellent	Presentations I Attend
46%	**Visuals (e.g., PowerPoint)**	19%
64%	**Handouts**	24%
64%	**Presenter Interacting with Audience**	24%
24%	**Presenter Having Audience Interact with Each Other**	8%
49%	**Overall Rating**	18%

Figure 2.4. How people rate themselves, vs. the presentations of others.

> The middle column shows the basic elements of a typical presentation. On the left, are the percentages of respondents who rated each item "good to excellent" for presentations they *give*. On the right are the percentages of respondents who rated these parts good to excellent for presentations they *attend*. As you can see, respondents consistently gave themselves higher marks, with nearly half believing their presentations fell into the good to excellent range overall. They were far less generous to their colleagues however, with less than a fifth earning good to excellent scores. These numbers suggest that audiences are frequently dissatisfied with what they see, but presenters simply aren't getting the message. (Goodman, 2005, p. 2)

How can you adopt a new mindset that will improve your business presentations? How can the business presentation platform be used to increase client conversion rates? The answer lies in putting the following three ideas into action:

1. Embrace change – the first step is to change your approach.
2. Reject the status quo – don't let today's practices hold you back.
3. Implement a holistic system – not just new tactics.

Now let's review each recommendation.

EMBRACE CHANGE

First things first. The cognitive approach to business presentations will require that you are open to change. I say this because in my early days of traveling the globe as a PowerPoint warrior, the entire company I worked for did presentations in the problem/solution, bullet-point, and 'bore-your-audience-to-death' format. How could I challenge the head of our sales and marketing departments on how we conducted business presentations?

It was only after ten years of personal and professional experience building my own successful businesses, presenting to hundreds of clients, tirelessly researching the subject in my doctoral dissertation, and winning awards such as Toastmasters International District 6 Champion of Public Speaking – it was only after all of those experiences that I learned – and what I learned can really be boiled down to this: presentations are *not* about you, the presenter. They are 100% about your audience. The idea of switching focus, style, and mindset is certainly a paradigm shift that must be done with your eyes wide open. Once you start being more 'customer centric' in business presentations, there's no going back. But first, you must be willing to make the change.

So what kind of change is needed? Consider the following:

- Find out how audiences optimally learn, and present to maximize their experience instead of just getting your information communicated.
- Invite audience participation so that you have conversations, not one-way presentations.
- Test and measure your progress using key performance indicators such as client feedback and conversion rates.

Consider the first point above. Take the use of bullet-points as an example. There is overwhelming scientific evidence that audiences don't respond optimally to excessive bullet-points – a hard habit to break amongst business presenters. Yet, like many presenters, I continued using them early on in my career until I really started focusing more on how audiences actually learn, and on what's most important to them. As a result of embracing this new way of presenting, I began making the changes that would meet my audiences' needs. One such change was in the area of using parables and pictures instead of bullet-points.

Here's an example of the scientific research against using excessive bullet-points. In the 1990s, professor Richard Mayer introduced an important concept called *the cognitive theory of multimedia learning*. In it, he described multimedia as any presentation involving the combination of words and text. His theory could be summed up in the following premises:

- The brain has only two 'channels' available for processing information; one is visual, and the other is auditory.

- Because the brain is actively processing at all times, there is a limit to how much it can actively handle in each channel.

Mayer's (2001) experiments involved showing two sets of slides to teach college students how lightning develops. The first set of slides were just images with no text, accompanied by a narrator explaining how lightning works. The second set, like most PowerPoint presentations today, had images, text and a narrator all happening at the same time.

Mayer found that the subjects in the image + narration only test retained 30% more than the subjects in the image + text + narration test. He also found that those subjects who viewed only the image and narration were 80% better at transferring the information they received and using it creatively in new situations.

(30% More Retention, 80% Better Transfer)

Image + Narration Only   **Image + Text + Narration**

Figure 2.5. Dr. Richard Mayer's Cognitive Theory of Multimedia

His conclusion was this; when you talk while simultaneously showing bullet-point text and images on the screen, you are forcing your clients' brains to do too much work, and their channels become overloaded. This is known as the *split attention principle* (Mayer & Moreno). It hinders the client's ability to understand your points, and it reduces your chance of influencing them to take action on your behalf.

> The **Split-Attention Principle:** "Students learn better when the instructional material does not require them to split their attention between multiple sources of mutually referring information."

The moral of this story is this: if you don't make the changes that will switch focus from you to your audience, you will never optimally connect with them. For me, it was important to learn the undisputed science against bullet-points in order to stop using them in presentations. Bullet-points are great for written text such as in a book like this one, but not for audiences in business presentations. Switching focus from me to my audience's needs made it much easier to embrace change overall. I have since done away with all of my bullet-point presentations, and I encourage you to do the same.

REJECT THE STATUS QUO

As you know, most professionals deliver presentations in a decidedly standard way, and they are not able to easily step outside of that particular box. The reasoning is usually something like, "If it ain't broke, don't fix it," right? However, as you can see from the surveys we discussed earlier, the problem is that people don't realize "it's" broken in the first place. They don't see the flaws in their own presentations, yet they are very clear about the poor performance of others. Here's an example outline of a typical problem/solution business presentation style:

- Agenda
- Our company
- Our Business Fit against the Customer's problem
- Our Solution's Features and benefits
- Action steps
- Any questions?

Does this resemble the presentation format in your organization? The challenge here is that most clients will tune you out somewhere between the agenda and your company overview. This example does not provide the audience much to awaken them emotionally, and is very much focused on 'our' company. The fundamental shift you have to make here is to think, not so much in terms of your customer research or your product knowledge, but rather in terms of the 'brains' to which you are speaking. How do brains respond to information? Does the nature of your information and delivery need to conform to the left-brain/right-brain architecture of the mind in order to be more easily accepted? *Yes!* Does your presentation have to conform to the most optimal way, or 'path of least resistance' by which your data will reach the brain's 'Aha!' center? *Yes!* Finally, do you have to build in the rules and laws of influence into your presentation through strategic stories, parables, examples, and even interactive, audience-participation games? *Yes!* And here's the biggie: How does suggesting that people ought to reserve questions till the end, when you'll say, "Any questions?" – how does that affect your listener's brains? You're basically telling them *not* to participate until you are done, and according to most research on how adults learn, that approach is 100% on the wrong track. If your listeners don't participate, they'll either fall asleep or privately tune you out while pretending to be listening.

IMPLEMENT A HOLISTIC SYSTEM

There was once a man who struggled with how to make more of his product, reduce the cost of production, and ensure that the quality and standards of each unit of his product were identical. His ultimate goal was to create an exceptional product that was accessible to all people at a great, affordable price. His competition continued to insist on making their products one at a time, by hand, so that they could continue to charge high prices. This man instead took some time off and invented a *system*. He invented a system that could multiply the effect of his workers' efforts in order to create a result that was much greater than the sum of its parts. The result was that this man took the market by storm, left the competition in the dust, sold millions of units of his product, and gave birth to an entirely new paradigm in the worldwide manufacturing industry. The man was Henry Ford, and his system was the assembly line, the conveyor belt, and ultimately, mass manufacturing as we know it today.

The power of having and using a system should not be underestimated. Having a repeatable, reliable process, as opposed to ad hoc, random tactics, is usually the difference between failure and success. If your goal is to be powerful and persuasive in business presentations all of the time, (as opposed to maybe sometimes), then you must do things as part of a cohesive, comprehensive system, different than what you have done so far. Instead of conforming to the way presentations are usually done, you must switch to an effective and reliable system for creating and delivering more interactive, influential audience experiences.

> A **system** ensures that your presentations will follow the rules of the cognitive mindset, and will be the best they can be each and every time.

This book presents the parable point presentation – which is an effective, field-proven system for creating, delivering, and measuring business presentations. Like Henry Ford's assembly line concept, you start each presentation from a template-driven, consistent messaging process that will ensure that you get your message right, and tell it right each time. You will learn how to create appropriate business stories and parables, and then systematically arrange them along a cognitive *BrainPath* with other multimedia elements for maximum audience persuasion. The parable point presentation system will help you make the cognitive switch to presentations that connect much better with your clients – because their brains will accept and assimilate your information with much less resistance.

CASE STUDY

THE PARABLE OF THE 'RIGHT' PROBLEM

I once heard an enchanting short parable about having the right mindset and addressing the right problems. Here it is, as written by Evelyn Genta:

Papa Josi was a farmer in Chietti, Italy. As this was what he knew how to do in the old country, this is what he did at his new home in the United States.

Papa Josi had a donkey, which he used to help around on the small farm. He named his donkey Scusi because the donkey always had an excuse for not working. He was eating ... he was tired ... he was visiting with the other farm animals. However, when Scusi did not want to work, Papa Josi would grab the donkey's face with his strong hands, look into the dark eyes and command "Scusi! Time-a-for getting-a-work-a!" After much persuasion, Scusi would finally allow himself to be led to the cart and would begin the tasks of the day.

One morning Papa Josi asked Evalina to bring Scusi out of the barn so that the work of the day could begin. Evalina took the worn leather lead attached to Scusi's harness and attempted to lead him outside. Scusi would not budge. First he dug his hoofs into the straw covered floor. Evalina pulled and pulled. Then, Scusi simply sat down. Evalina went to Scusi's backside and began pushing him screaming ... "Move Scusi ... get up Scusi!" She pushed and pushed and continued pushing at his backside.

Papa Josi, hearing the commotion, came into the barn. Looking at the situation, he said in his very Italian voice "Evalina ... why-a-you-a-speakin' to the donkey's ass-a, when-a-you should-a-be-speakin' to the donkey's head-a?"

Solving life's problems can be simple or complex. Often, however, it is a matter of having the right mindset, and determining what the real problem is.

(By Evelyn Genta.)

CHAPTER 2 SUMMARY

THE COGNITIVE PRESENTATION MINDSET

- There are essentially two approaches to business presentations. One is the standard problem/solution format, and the other is to design presentations that work the way brains work – a cognitive mindset for business presentations.

- Most people don't realize how bad their presentations are, but they are very aware of other people's bad presentations.

- In order to adopt a mindset that will improve your business presentations, you must embrace change, reject the status quo, and implement a holistic system.

EXERCISES

- Take a look at your current, go-to-market business presentation. Review at a high level, its format, or 'flow'. Do you notice the problem/solution/features approach? Have you built into this presentation the cognitive aspect of how brains function? Does your presentation address both the logical and emotional centers of the brain?

- Redesign your presentation into three distinct sections and make a concerted effort to offer your audience an experience that follows the format: (a) awaken emotions, (b) exchange stories, and (c) deliver 'Aha!'

3. Your Biggest Presentation Challenge – Is You

> *"A man's greatest battle is the one he fights with himself."*
> *- IGBO PROVERB*

O nce upon a time, there was a wise old man who lived at the crossroads between two villages, one in a valley, and the other on a mountain. One day, a young man arrived at the crossroads on his way up the mountain and declared: "Old man, I am sick and tired of the village in the valley. The people there are all self-centered, shallow, unfriendly, and greedy. Do you know if it is different up there in the mountains?" The old man replied: "Alas, I think you will find it to be the same as the village in the valley." Dejected, the young traveler continued on his journey - up toward the village in the mountains.

Later that day another young traveler arrived at the crossroads on his way down to the valley village. He struck up a conversation with the old man, saying, "My life has been great up there in the mountain village. I made many friends, and so many people were good to me. Do you know much about the village in the valley below? How will I find it there?"

And the old man said, "Young man, I think you will find the village in the valley to be exactly like the village in the mountains." With a smile on his face, the young traveler left the crossroads and headed toward the village in the valley (Knight, 2005, p. 28).

The parable above illustrates how in life, what you get is based on what you're looking for and your attitude towards it. This is what I call paradigmatic interpretation. Your paradigm is like a lens, and it determines how you see the world. For example, if you put on a pair of blue lenses, you would probably interpret most things as having a shade of blue in them, while the rest of us, (without the blue lenses), would see things in their true colors. But if for some reason you were to suddenly take those blue lenses off, you would all of a sudden see what we see, and your perspective on everything would change. You would experience what Thomas Kuhn succinctly defined as a "paradigm shift" (Kuhn, 1996).

Visualize a scene from when people thought the world was flat. Can you imagine how they must have perceived the mad man who excitedly suggested that the world was round? The *idea* of a flat earth was an example of a paradigm, and it prevailed for many years until Columbus was able to travel far enough to prove that the world was in fact round, or more precisely stated, elliptical. When people finally accepted this new reality, a paradigm shift occurred in their minds, changing their perception of reality from the old, flat world, to an elliptical one with limitless possibilities.

The first step in your journey toward influencing audiences to buy whatever you sell - starts with none other than **YOU**! You must examine and clarify your own prevailing business paradigms; however, there is a catch - paradigms are usually *hidden*!

Take for example, the prevailing hidden paradigm – in which PowerPoint presentations are the norm – which results in the creation and daily delivery of millions of boring, bullet-point presentations. Certainly nobody wakes up excitedly each morning and announces; "Boy, I'm gonna bore people silly today!" The fact is simply this: You can't always see your 'blue lenses' when you're wearing them. This is not an easy task; consider the popular saying; "It is hard to see the picture when you are in the frame." It is usually easier for an outsider to help you see the paradigm under which you operate.

> The reason there are millions of non-persuasive, ineffective business presentations each day is that most people operate from three **hidden**, personal presentation paradigms:
>
> 1. The CUSTOMER paradigm
> 2. The PURPOSE paradigm
> 3. The LEADERSHIP paradigm

Your customer paradigm is your answer to the question: "Do I habitually operate and communicate from my point of view, or from my customer's?" Your purpose paradigm is the answer to the question: "What is the prevailing purpose in my mind when I give business presentations?" Finally, your leadership paradigm is essentially your leadership communication style, which is the answer to the question, "How I do lead?"

By the way, have you ever stopped to ask yourself these questions? If you haven't, you are not alone. Most people haven't either. However, herein lies your challenge: if you intend to become more influential in business presentations, you will have to start by thinking differently. You will have to take off your current lenses, and experience a paradigm shift in the way you think about business presentations. The goal of this chapter is to help you challenge your own three hidden business paradigms. As Einstein's popular saying goes, "we cannot solve problems with the same thinking that created them." Right? Okay, so let's get started!

1. WHAT IS YOUR CUSTOMER PARADIGM?

Imagine that you are a reporter and you work at WSG-AM, an all-news talk radio station. One day a friend of yours is driving home, listening to a car radio that has been damaged, and only tunes to WII-FM. What if a heavy storm is approaching, and you want to make sure she finds this out in a timely manner? What if you do the best you can, which is to keep broadcasting feverishly on your AM station, in the hope that she will somehow hear it? Do you think she will ever hear you? Probably not, because, as we said earlier, her tuner is stuck on WII-FM!

That radio station, WII-FM, is the one most people in your audience are biologically hardwired to listen to, and it stands for the question: "What's In It For Me?" Ironically, when *you* give business presentations you are also hardwired to look out for yourself and your product's interests, so the tendency is for you to continue broadcasting on WSG-AM – "What's So Great About Me!" This is an illustration of the hidden *customer* paradigm, which is one of the most destructive paradigms in all of business.

Even though so many people claim that they are customer-centric in outlook, they are simply not consciously aware that they are operating from a ME point of view. Their customer paradigm is evidenced by the kinds of questions that run through their heads during sales interactions:

How can this situation benefit ME?
How can I grow MY business?
How can I get these customers to buy MY products?

If these questions dominate your thinking, then it will inadvertently spill over in your communication. As a result, this hidden paradigm stops many business people from creating truly customer-focused services; it stops managers and entrepreneurs from building teams with other leaders; and it also stops business presenters from creating and delivering truly audience-centered, persuasive presentations.

Unfortunately, most presenters simply talk past their audiences. Like two people speaking different languages without a translator, business presentations can go on for hours without anyone truly hearing or caring about what the speaker is saying. If you want your presentations to be persuasive, to hold audience attention, and to inspire people to take action in favor of whatever you're selling, you have to learn to broadcast on their WII-FM station, instead of on your WSG-AM station. Instead of leading off your discussion points from your product or service point of view, why not make the same points from the viewpoint of your customers' *problems?* Instead of saying, "Here are all the fantastic, wonderful features and benefits of our product," why not ask, "Can you tell me more about the problems you are dealing with?" The former is about ME, and GETTING, while the latter is about CUSTOMERS and

GIVING. The former is broadcasting from WSG-AM, while the latter is asking for and sending signals on the WII-FM station. Obviously, the latter approach will get solid business results, whereas the former will continue to result in bored, tired, uninspired audiences.

When you first meet a prospect, how do you answer the following question?

"What do you do?"

If your answer to the above question is something like these:

"I am a technical product manager,"

"I'm the Vice President of Marketing at an enterprise software company"

You are describing what you *do*, not what your prospects or clients *benefit* from you. This sort of answer will not engage your prospect, and you won't get them thinking about their own self-focused interests. This kind of response is what most people habitually provide. It is a 'ME' focused response, and is not as successful as a WII-FM approach. A WII-FM approach might be:

"I help fortune 500 clients increase their profits through reliable information-sharing with their partners, suppliers, and customers."

Remember, people are biologically predisposed to taking care of their own interests above all else, so, help them do that. Give them the gift of caring for their issues and you will reap the benefit of them caring about yours. When you tailor *all* your speech habits to a WII-FM approach, your business presentations will become much more effective. Your audiences will be inspired to action, because you've presented everything in terms of their best interests. Having a customer paradigm requires that you are a GIVER, and that you always start from the customer's point of view:

"Give what you want to receive" – *Robert Cialdini*

The self-centered, 'ME' focused paradigm is very difficult to identify and tackle, because it is so deeply rooted and ingrained in many of us. I often explain it by using a very simple parable. You may have heard of Spencer Johnson's "Who Moved My Cheese?" – one of the greatest and most lighthearted business parables of all time. Dr. Johnson used that parable to illustrate the concept of handling change in life and business. His story is one of the greatest examples of how to use business parables to make points. In a similar manner, I like to use a very lighthearted parable to explain this idea of self-centeredness in business. Following is an example of a parable I developed to explain the 'ME' phenomenon. It is one of the more fun parables in my repertoire, and it is derived from an ancient West African folktale. I call it 'The Parable of ME':

Once upon a time there was a great famine in the land. All the animals went over to get help from their two leaders, turtle and butterfly. Turtle explained that he had just registered a new business called *ME* Incorporated, and its purpose was to transport all the animals to heaven, where God would be obliged to provide them with food. Everyone thought it was a brilliant idea except for one thing: how would they get to heaven? Luckily, butterfly volunteered to provide wings to everyone for free, and as soon as everyone had wings, they were off to heaven.

When they got to the gates of heaven, turtle shouted, "Stop! We cannot enter heaven without having names. It is disrespectful to God!" So all the animals picked names, but when it got to turtle's turn, he decided to call himself a strange name: *Olive View*. All the animals found his name comical. After all, what on earth did a view of olives have to do with anything? They ignored turtles new name, and went on into heaven.

Finally, God arrived and spread out food for miles, and the animals prepared to jump in and have the feast of their lives. But before they could start eating, turtle shouted, "Stop! We cannot eat until we ask God who He brought this food for! It is disrespectful to God!" He then turned and politely asked God to kindly tell them for whom He had brought this wonderful meal. God replied:

"I brought this food for ... all of you!"

Doesn't that sound like turtle's new name? You guessed it! You can probably imagine what happened next. The turtle ate up all the food and left all the animals hungry. So in anger, the animals seized his wings and pushed him out of heaven, and he fell to the ground and broke his back in a thousand pieces. That is why, till today, the turtle has a broken back.

However, God took pity on the animals and made an important announcement. He said, "Go back to the world, and give this altruistic butterfly one dollar per day so that he can give you wings to return to heaven for your daily bread. Whenever I see you, I will feed you!"

So the animals did exactly that, and very soon, the butterfly's wing-manufacturing empire grew so successful, that he renamed it *Microsoft*, and became the richest living thing on earth!

(Adapted from an Igbo folktale)

The Parable of ME showcases the turtle displaying one of the most destructive hidden paradigms in business today. It teaches that there are at least two paradigms for the way we live and do business. The ME paradigm is what the turtle was afflicted with, where everything was always about him. The CUSTOMER paradigm was displayed by the butterfly, who knew that in life and business, it is really all about satisfying the customer. When your business presentation is all about you, there is no room for the audience. Part of the reason your listeners may feel disconnected is that they were never involved in the first place. Your name was *Olive View*, and you ate the *food* all by yourself!

Your goal as an inspirational, influential business presenter is to create a **100% customer-centered experience**, and you cannot do this effectively if you are operating from the paradigm of ME.

Ask yourself – in business – do you operate from the paradigm of ME, or the CUSTOMER paradigm? The paradox in business presentations is that the presenter is usually trying to GET a sale while the audience is also trying to GET something for themselves. Since both parties are looking for ways to GET, no one is GIVING anything! And yet, one of the most powerful laws of influence in the universe is reciprocity. If you want to *get* something, you have to *give* something first. What can you give in a business presentation? How about giving audience members a chance to be heard? You will be surprised at how much greater the opportunity for influence becomes when the customer gets involved and tells *their* story.

2. WHAT IS THE PURPOSE OF YOUR PRESENTATIONS?

Have you ever seen the movie *Braveheart?* It's a powerful movie about how the Scottish fought the British relentlessly under the leadership of renegade outlaw William Wallace. Like most medieval war movies, there is always the inspirational speech given by the leader before the battle. He reminds the fighters about *what* they are fighting for, telling them, "It's a great day to die today!" What if just before they charge off to certain death, a small voice in the audience pierces through the propaganda and asks *why?* "Why exactly are we fighting this war again?

That simple question – *why* – is the question of purpose. In order to survive and achieve long-term success, most businesses develop clearly stated vision, mission, and strategy statements for achieving their organizational goals. The vision statement essentially answers the question, "where are we going?" The mission statement then answers the question, "what are we going to do along the way?" Finally, the strategy statement answers the question "how are we going to get there?"

However, there is usually something implied but markedly missing. "*Why* are we going there in the first place?" This is the question of purpose, and it is the cohesive glue that gives sustainability to the rest of the other statements. Similarly, a business presentation should be clear in terms of its vision, mission, and strategy, but it must also have a central purpose. Your understanding, hidden or otherwise, of the central purpose of a business presentation, guides everything you do when you are presenting – whether you know it or not. Everyone has a purpose for what they do, because it shows in their actions and results. The person who wakes up, does nothing all day, and then says she has no purpose in life is not telling you the whole truth. Her purpose is actually quite clear: her purpose is to do nothing all day!

Exercise: Before you read any further, take out a piece of paper and write down in one sentence, what you think the central **purpose** of a business presentation is ... Why do you give Business Presentations? When you're done, read on.

Most people see business presentations as an opportunity to transfer product information to prospective clients in the form of features and benefits. In fact, most of our management schools and sales training programs have perpetuated this limiting definition, and it has hurt many aspiring executives, salespeople, and entrepreneurs immeasurably. Here's a popular definition, according to Moncrief and Shipp (1997):

> The objective of a sales presentation is to convince the prospect or customer that the seller's product and product attributes can satisfy the customer's needs better than can those of the competition . . . Sales presentations are typically constructed around the product features and the benefits that they provide, or specific customer needs. (p. 169)

I am going to guess that your definition was similar to that one. If so, you are partially right. The problem with this definition is that it is a 'ME' paradigm definition. It is about GETTING more clients, and it does not stem from, or fully consider the client's point of view. Saying you want to satisfy customers is not enough; you have to deeply believe it, and practice it in everything you do. How can one think differently, as Einstein might say, in order to get different and *better* results? How can one shift away from this paradigm in order to open up new possibilities in the quest to inspire audiences to action?

Here's the paradigm shift:

The purpose of a business presentation is to earn or confirm **trust**, encourage audience **participation** through sharing stories, and create an **'Aha!'** experience in the minds of your listeners.

The combination of these leads to an increase in your ability to influence your prospective clients.

Cognitive science tells us that there are two distinct ways in which the human brain solves problems. One is the straightforward logical approach, and the other is a heightened emotional state of insight called 'Aha!' This experience was first credited to Archimedes as he discovered something profound and shouted, "Eureka!" It is a moment of breakthrough and illumination. When a client gets this feeling of 'Aha!' during your business presentation, they find insight, they 'get it'. They will truly understand how your solution solves their problems, and you have moved them much closer to making a decision in your favor. We will revisit this topic in chapter 7, (The Brain's Secret Path to 'Aha!'), but for now, it is important to understand that if clients don't 'get' what you are saying – if they never experience 'Aha!' – then it will be very difficult to move them to a decision, regardless of what other tools you have in your sales arsenal.

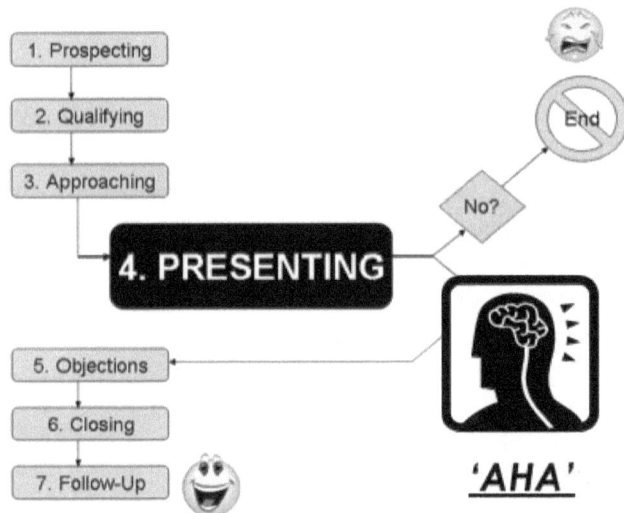

Figure 4.1. Purpose of a presentation: to share stories that create *'Aha!'*

Consider your standard relationship sales cycle in Figure 4.1. The business presentation phase is arguably the most critical stage in the entire process. As you build relationships and learn more about your prospect, you have that one important chance at getting them to *'Aha!'* If you miss that opportunity, the entire campaign, and all the money, time, and effort spent on it could be irretrievably lost. However, if you can get them to that point of deep insight, you can move to the next stage, which is hopefully asking for the order, and closing the deal!

3. WHAT'S YOUR LEADERSHIP PARADIGM?

The angry CEO charged into the office carrying his big stick, and in a loud voice, declared that if he discovered one more mistake in the design prototype, everyone would get fired – and he meant it too! Everyone from the janitor all the way up to the Vice President of Production would be gone today if they made any more mistakes. Suddenly, as quickly as he had stormed in, he sat down in the middle of the reception area, dropped his stick, and pulled out a carrot. He replaced his angry voice with a calm, low tone so that everyone had to listen carefully: "Whoever is first in meeting the new deadline tomorrow, with the least quality defects, gets a trip to Hawaii and a 5% raise in their salary! And whoever has the most mistakes gets fired as an example to all!" With that, he left the room as quickly as he had arrived.

Everyone was petrified. Everything was on the line! As the boss stormed off – back to finish his round of golf with the other bosses in the neighborhood – the Vice President of Production called a quick, desperate meeting. Once everyone gathered together he said:

> *"Today we have seen that the road ahead of us is rife with difficulty. Yet we know that we can do this. Our families depend on us to do the best we can. We must work together to reach heights of both personal and group success. If we achieve our goals, regardless of how we do it, I will forfeit my salary this month to buy everyone that trip to Hawaii. I will make the coffee, go buy Chinese take-out, and I will not leave this building until the last of you has found a way to make this a successful product release. We are all in this together!"*

The workers felt uplifted. Together, they proceeded courageously, and were successful in meeting their quality and deadline requirements.

Communication is the ultimate conduit of leadership. The way you communicate is usually congruent with the way you lead, and a business presentation is one of those opportunities where you get a chance to showcase your most effective leadership style. In every business meeting, your audience is looking to you for effective leadership. Will you be a dictator, or a facilitator? The examples above are two extremes of leadership communication styles on display. If you consider these two extremes as part of a continuum of styles, transactional leadership will represent the least effective, while transformational leadership represents the most effective.

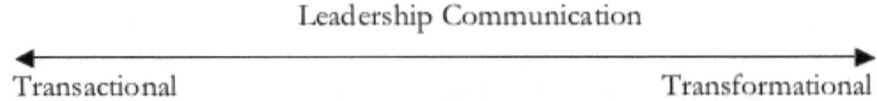

Figure 4.2. The Two Leadership Communication Paradigms

Consider Figure 4.2: on the left is a transactional leadership style, and on the right is a transformational leadership style. The transactional leader, the boss, was simply offering an *exchange* – you do a good job, and this is your reward. You do a bad job, and that is your punishment. This form of leadership has been shown in both research and practice to be very ineffective in the long run (Burns, 1979). People may do what you want them to because they have a gun pressed against their heads, but the moment they have a chance, they will run far away from you.

The second style, transformational leadership, is not focused on rewards and exchanges. Rather, it starts by first considering the needs and motivations of your followers, and from that vantage point, it focuses on establishing a shared vision. If you start from *their* vantage point, you are more able to inspire them to actions they may never have considered on their own. Some of the greatest leaders of our times, such as Gandhi, Martin Luther King, and Nelson Mandela, are transformational leaders, who raise the level of inspiration, transforming everyone positively in the process (Bass, 1990).

Which kind of leader are you? As Aristotle once said, "we *are* what we repeatedly do." When you run a business meeting, are you there to dictate one-way information while implying rewards and punishments? (The extreme being something like; "buy my product or else your company won't be successful! If you go with the competition, I'll be here next year to pick up your failed initiatives!") Or are you uplifting minds, building up emotions, and pushing the envelope of possibilities? Are you involving the audience in a communal discovery of collective greatness or are you doing all the talking? This is an important personal question for you to ask and to answer. However, one thing is clear. If you run your business meetings from a transformational leadership stand point, you will create more inspired followers of your message, who will in turn spread your parables to others. So, tell parables, and listen actively to your client's stories. Instead of delivering one-way, 'ME' focused transactional talks, your goal should be to adopt the mindset of a transformational leader and communicator, able to get deep into the hearts of listeners.

Stories are the ultimate leadership persuasion tool. In 1995, Harvard professor Howard Gardner wrote a fascinating book entitled, *Leading Minds: An anatomy of Leadership*, in which he claimed that the central function of a leader is to be a good storyteller (Gardner & Laskin, 1995). In his thesis, what leaders really do is tell *stories*, which in our context, translates to stories that must make benefit points to an audience. Leaders use words as well as their lives to convey stories that directly or indirectly influence others to action. In Gardner's definition, direct leaders such as Roosevelt and Churchill are joined by indirect leaders such as Albert Einstein and Martin Luther King. Although Einstein and King held no political office, their influence on others, on humanity, was immense to say the least. Gardner also talks about how the stories these leaders tell must wrestle with the stories already in the minds of followers, and how a leader's stories must win the battle in order for the leader to be successful.

On a smaller but equally important scale, the same can be said of anyone conducting a business presentation. For the brief time that you have the podium, you, the presenter, are looked upon as an indirect leader, and your major tool of influence is the *story* you tell, not necessarily the information you share. Your audience is looking to you for leadership, guidance, and assurance that the vision you paint is achievable. You have a unique opportunity to influence people in ways that a one-on-one conversation could never achieve because you have the simulated leadership power of the podium. Your story must battle the stories that already exist in their heads, and influence their perceptions of reality with respect to your product or service. If they believe and trust you, they will be inspired to take action that is congruent with your vision.

CASE STUDY

A PARABLE FOR INSPIRING CHANGE

As a program director at the world bank (Washington, D.C.) in the mid-1990s, Stephen Denning was at a loss for how to convince his colleagues of the value of knowledge management. Presentations built on solid research and carefully constructed PowerPoint slides got him nowhere. Then he started telling this simple story:

In June of last year, a health worker in a tiny town in Zambia went to the Web site of the Centers for Disease Control and got an answer to a question about the treatment of malaria. Remember that this was in Zambia, one of the poorest countries in the world, and it was in a tiny place six hundred kilometers from the capitol city. But the most striking thing about this picture, at least for us, is that the World Bank isn't in it. Despite our know-how on all kinds of poverty-related issues, that knowledge isn't available to the millions of people who could use it. Imagine if it were. Think what an organization we could become.

This narrative succeeded in persuading Denning's listeners to envision a broader, more ambitious future for the organization. It succeeded where analysis and argument had failed. "Analysis might excite the mind, but it hardly offers a route to the heart. And that's where you must go if you are to motivate people not only to take action but to do so with energy and enthusiasm," writes Denning in *The Leader's Guide to Storytelling: Mastering the Art and Discipline of Business Narrative* (John Wiley & Sons, 2005).

Denning, now a knowledge management and organizational storytelling consultant, argues that effective leadership requires the ability to choose the right story at the right time and tell it well. His book dispenses thoughtful advice for leaders who want their words to work powerfully on their behalf.

(Phoel, 2006, p. 3)

CHAPTER 3 SUMMARY

YOUR BIGGEST PRESENTATION CHALLENGE – IS YOU!

- A Paradigm is a way of looking at the world, and is like a lens through which you see things. Your response to the world, and activities within it, are shaped largely by the beliefs, assumptions, and paradigms that you hold.

- Paradigms are usually hidden. Because they are not immediately obvious, people struggle to understand why they take certain actions, and why they get certain results.

- The first step in your journey to persuasive business presentations is to expose, understand and clarify your own hidden paradigms.

- The hidden business paradigms people struggle with are:
    o The CUSTOMER paradigm
    o The PRESENTATION paradigm
    o The LEADERSHIP paradigm

- You are either operating from a 'ME' paradigm or a 'CUSTOMER' paradigm. Make sure it is the latter in your business presentations.

- The purpose of a business presentation is NOT just to convince people to buy – it is to exchange stories in order to help them reach a state of *'Aha!'* – which will ultimately lead your clients closer to a decision in your favor.

- You are either a transactional leader, or a transformational leader. The former exchanges rewards and punishments, while the latter inspires followers to greatness. People respond more favorably in the long term to the latter. You are playing a leadership role in presentations, so make sure you are transformational, not just transactional.

EXERCISES

- Write down in one sentence, your answer to the question, "What do you do?" Refine it until it is just right. (Be careful of your customer paradigm as you do this!)

- Take a look at your last few business presentations. In what ways (specifically) did you intentionally try to earn trust? Write it down. Were you successful?

- In what ways did you get the audience involved in those recent presentations? Write them down. Did the audience willingly participate?

- In what ways did you get them to "aha"? What specific explanation, story, phrase etc. did you use to achieve that result? Write that down also.

4. The Brain's Secret Path To 'Aha!'

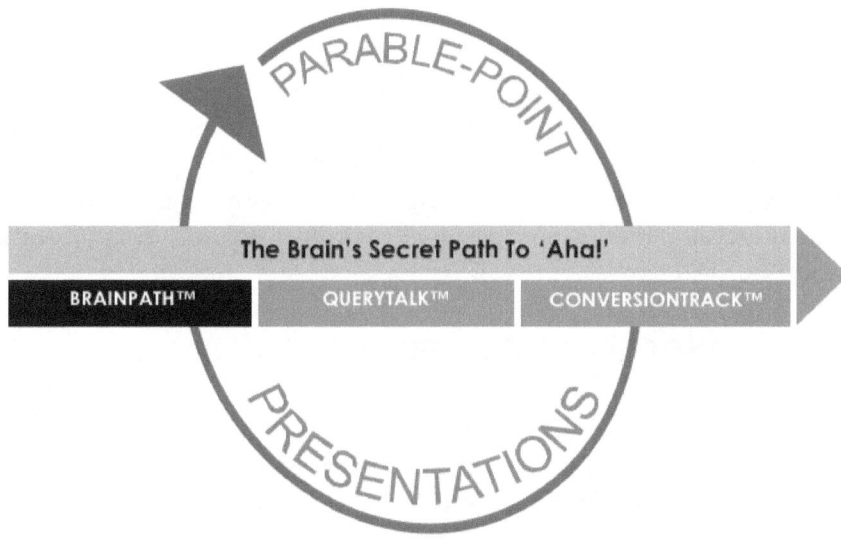

"If I supply you with a thought, you may remember it and you may not; but if I can make you think a thought yourself, I have indeed added to your stature."

- ELBERT HUBBARD

The goal of a business presentation is to help your audience achieve a whole-brained *breakthrough* in the way they perceive your product or service. This breakthrough, or 'Aha!' moment, is the point at which the perception gap we've described earlier is closed. It is the critical point at which a listener ceases to view your product's features as something you are 'selling' them, and begins to immediately see it as something they need in order to achieve their own personal and professional goals. This breakthrough is the critical moment of truth that you should strive for, and the process of guiding your clients to that moment is called perception management. If you are unable to manage your clients' perceptions to that point of clarity and breakthrough, you will not receive any decision in your favor, and there will be no signing on the dotted line. Given the plethora of influence strategies and tactics that are available, how does one bring them all together in a business presentation to achieve 'Aha!' in the clients' minds? How do you close he perception gap? This chapter delivers the answer to that question. You will discover that there is a proven path to that ecstatic point of influence where your client's needs are exactly in lock step with your offering. Getting to *'Aha!'* is something that is best achieved through a presentation model I call *BrainPath* – the path of least resistance to influence in the mind of a client. BrainPath requires only one simple change in how you present your facts: turn as many of them as you can into memorable parables, and arrange them in a manner that appeals to the way your listeners' brains will accept them.

THE PARADOX OF TRUTH AND PARABLE

The secret power of parables – their ability to help you with perception management – can be found in their capability to go where facts cannot – into the emotional mind, where they are understood, remembered, and used for decision-making. Consider the story of 'Truth and Parable', a popular Jewish tale taken from Beatrice Silverman Weinreich's *Yiddish Folktales*:

> The great scholar known as Vilna Gaon once asked the Preacher of Dubno, "Help me understand, what makes a parable so influential? If I recite Torah there is a small audience, but let me tell a parable and the synagogue is full. Why is that?" The *dubner maged* replied, "I'll explain it to you by means of a parable.
>
> "Once upon a time, Truth went about the streets as naked as the day he was born. As a result, no one would let him into their homes. Whenever people caught sight of him, they turned away and fled. One day when Truth was sadly wandering about, he came upon Parable. Now, Parable was dressed in splendid clothes of beautiful colors. And Parable, seeing Truth, said, 'Tell me, neighbor, what makes you look so sad?' Truth replied bitterly, 'Ah, brother, things are bad. Very bad. I'm old, very old, and no one wants to acknowledge me. No one wants anything to do with me.'
>
> "Hearing that, Parable said, 'People don't run away from you because you're old. I too am old. Very old. But the older I get, the better people like me. I'll tell you a secret: Everyone likes things disguised and prettied up a bit. Let me lend you some splendid

clothes like mine, and you'll see that the very people who pushed you aside will invite you into their homes and be glad of your company.'

Truth took Parable's advice and put on the borrowed clothes. And from that time on, Truth and Parable have gone hand in hand together and everyone loves them. They make a happy pair. (Weinreich, 1988)

This analogy points to 'truth' as your (logical) product fact or feature, and 'parable' as the short story you use to dress it up for maximum assimilation by your audience. Parables are a potent vehicle for conveying customer benefit points. Parables and benefit points go hand in hand like salt and pepper; you need both for a well-rounded taste. Benefits alone would be naked, unattractive, and lacking in emotional connection. By themselves, Parables would be confusing. One without the other would be insufficient to create the magic 'Aha!' that is so important in inspirational learning. The power of the parable point presentation system lies in this duality. By setting up a parable, you build a world that carries an emotional message; by following it with its customer-benefit point, you concurrently satisfy a listener's logical brain, ensuring the highest possibility of persuasive, whole-brained impact for your message. This is why we talk in terms of 'parable points'. First you tell the parable, and then you make the point. The parable is an example or analogy that opens up your mind and makes you think, thereby allowing the benefit point to truly hit home.

Always tell the truth in a business parable, or else you are simply telling tall tales, which will not advance your cause. The power of parables is that they represent truth – *cognitively* arranged!

Miriam Webster defines Parable as derived from the Greek 'paraballein' which means 'to compare'. Parables do not exist by themselves; rather, they come as a pair with your offering's benefit point. Parables allow the presenter to quickly gain the all-important attention of the audience, while the point remains temporarily hidden. Meanwhile, the listeners are transported to a place where self-armament is dropped; defenses are reduced while truth is allowed to follow. Almost like a Trojan horse, the benefit point becomes more purely and easily digested by the listener, and the state of 'Aha!' becomes much more accessible.

ARISTOTLE'S RHETORIC: THE PATH TO 'AHA!'

More than two thousand years ago, Aristotle indirectly alluded to the idea of a natural pathway to influence in his seminal work, *Rhetoric*. His timeless premises still hold true today in any form of perception management or persuasive communication in business. In his seminal work, Aristotle defined rhetoric as a universal art of persuasion that depends on the interaction of three factors: the speaker, the hearer, and the subject matter itself. As such, he proposed three ways in which persuasion is achieved:

> Of the modes of persuasion furnished by the spoken word there are three kinds. The first kind depends on the personal character of the speaker; the second on putting the audience into a certain frame of mind; the third on the proof, or apparent proof, provided by the words of the speech itself. (Aristotle, 350 BC, chap. 2)

Not much has changed in the human condition since Aristotle wrote these timeless words. He was describing the importance of ethos (personal credibility), logos (logic), and pathos (listeners' emotions) in achieving influence in presentations.

1. **Ethos**: the personal credibility of the speaker.

2. **Pathos**: Putting the audience in a certain frame of mind.

3. **Logos**: Proof from the logic of the words.

Figure 7.1. Aristotle's Rhetorical Triad

With the advent of neuro-imaging, we can now demonstrate visually how the brain works, invariably confirming what Aristotle theorized so many years ago. Aristotle's theory described *what* must be done to gain influence in presentations, but new discoveries in science teach us *how* to go about doing it. For example, we now know, based on studies done about how adults learn best, that the way to achieve Aristotle's Pathos (putting the audience in a certain frame of mind) is by getting people to participate and experience the learning process themselves. Also, we now know that the brain responds more favorably to content that is both logical *and* emotional.

The Brain's path to 'Aha!' is the same as it has always been since Aristotle's time, but thanks to neuroscience, instead of just knowing 'what' to do, we now know 'how' to do it as well. BrainPath is a synthesis of Aristotle's original triad of Ethos, Logos, and Pathos, with our newfound revelations of 'how' to achieve them. The BrainPath model for 'how' to persuade during presentations is therefore represented by the categories of *trust, participation,* and *'Aha!'* These are the brain's gateposts, which you must traverse in the minds of your audience in order for you to reach their decision-making centers.

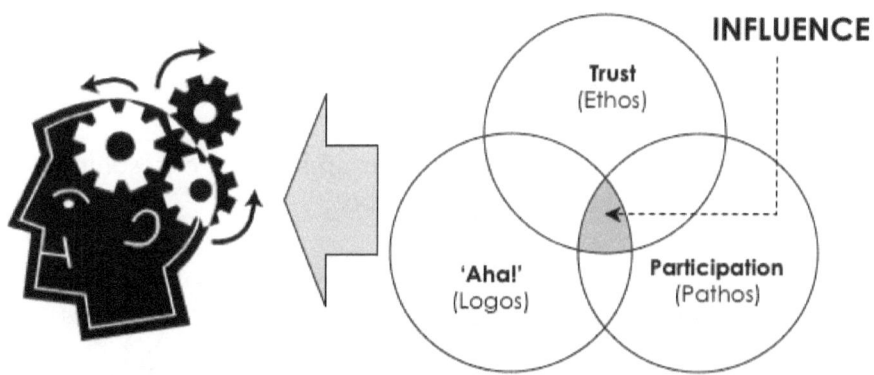

Figure 7.2. Influence is the confluence of Trust, Participation, and 'Aha!'

Figure 7.2 shows influence as the result of three intersecting circles, which represent the three brain reactions you must elicit from your audience. The confluence of these three responses produces the desired purpose of a business presentation – to inspire action.

In order to persuade, a business presentation must elicit three brain responses from your audience: They must **trust** you, **participate** with you in the presentation, and experience "**Aha!**"

Aristotle's Triad	Description	How it's done
Ethos	The speaker's credibility.	Win **Trust** and create a comfortable learning environment.
Pathos	Putting the audience in a certain frame of mind.	Encourage **Participation** from the audience.
Logos	Making logical arguments.	Use storytelling and perception management to deliver audience '**Aha**!'

The Audience Must Trust You

The primary requirement for achieving influence in a presentation is that the audience must trust you. This level of trust in the minds of your audience should be so pertinent that they will emerge from your presentation as *disciples* of your core message. Your best tools for achieving this are stories and parables.

The Audience Must Participate With You

Adults learn best when they participate and figure out solutions for themselves as part of the learning experience.

What I hear, I forget. What I hear and see, I remember a little. What I hear, see, and ask questions about or discuss with someone else, I begin to understand. What I hear, see, discuss and do, I acquire knowledge and skill. What I teach to another, I master. – Confucius

Your presentation must have visual, audio, and kinesthetic elements in order to capture the full involvement of your audience. One important thing to do in every presentation is to ask people to participate, and consistently ask them questions to elicit involvement. Ask them to tell you stories of their challenges, or involve them in interactive games to drive home certain points. You have to get people thinking and solving puzzles along with you, or else they may tune you out.

The Audience Must Experience "Aha!"

Finally, in order to be moved to action, your audience must reach that place of enlightenment and understanding that is extraordinary. Ever since Archimedes shouted "Eureka" after solving a scientific riddle, people have described these moments of extreme *insight* and revelation as "Aha!" moments. Essentially, when a person solves a problem and feels like a light bulb just went off in their heads, they have experienced a revelatory or 'Aha!' moment. One word of caution, you must make sure that the 'Aha!' experience you try to create in the audience is based on solving *their* problems, not touting your own features and benefits, or else you will have defeated the purpose.

"There can be no knowledge without emotion. We may be aware of a truth, yet until we have felt its force, it is not ours. To the cognition of the brain must be added the experience of the soul."

- Arnold Bennett

BRAINPATH - THE KEY TO INFLUENCE

Yale professor Paul D. MacLean is famous for having proposed the triune theory of the brain – the notion that we are really three brains in one, (reptilian, limbic, and neo-cortex), divided neatly along the lines of how our brains developed during evolution. This triune theory of the brain has since been leveraged widely in the fields of physiology, psychiatry and brain research. According to this view of the brain, each of the three sections 'grew' over time as humankind evolved in response to the needs of survival. (Figure 7.3)

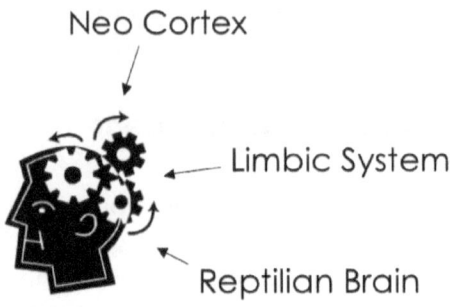

Neo Cortex

Limbic System

Reptilian Brain

Figure 7.3. The Triune Theory of the Brain

The first, original brain in the process of evolution is the *reptilian* brain, sometimes called the 'R complex'; this is the portion of the brain that we have in common with reptiles and birds. This brain was developed to handle basic needs such as hunger, temperature control, the 'fight, flight, or fear' responses when danger approached, and so on. When confronted with any stimulus, the reptilian brain works by essentially asking the question:

"Am I safe?"

If the answer is yes, the body will remain relaxed. This reptilian brain also deals with the issue of trust. As discussed earlier, trust must be earned as a prerequisite to influence. In a business presentation there are really only two feelings the audience can experience – comfort or nervousness. The way to answer the question of trust is to use a parable that explains *who* you are, *why* you are here, and why the audience should feel comfortable listening to you. This is what we will describe in chapter ten as 'the parables of 'who' and 'why' – your story for who you are, and why anyone in the audience should care. This is how you earn the right to speak.

As people evolved further, we didn't get rid of this reptilian brain. Instead, a new, more advanced brain grew on top of it in response to our evolutionary needs. As our brains became more complex, the next area that developed was the *limbic* system, which is the place where our emotions are kept. We share this brain with animals such as dogs and cats, which are able to experience "feelings" as well. This feeling brain contains the *amygdala*, the central gateway of emotions. The limbic system always asks the questions:

"How do I feel?"
"Does this person care about me?'
"Am I interested in this discussion?"

The way to get people connected to your points at the limbic level is to get them involved. As we discussed in chapter three, you must get people to participate in the discussion so that it is not only about you. Once they feel as though they are determining the outcome of the discussion, they become empowered and more receptive to your information. Remember, no one cares what you say as much as what they say themselves. The customer is always right, so let them come to their own conclusions through participating in your presentation.

Finally, as we became sentient, 'feeling and thinking' beings, the cortex grew and surrounded the rest of the brain. This particular layer of the brain is unique to primates and most advanced in humans. It allows us to make complex decisions and calculations that dogs and cats are unable to make. When we receive information from the outside world, it has to travel along the evolutionary BrainPath, climbing from the reptilian brain, to the limbic system, and finally into the cortex, where a final decision is made. This is where the brain asks:

"Do I feel 'Aha!'?"

If the brain feels 'Aha!' it becomes much more predisposed to influence and finally understands the value of what is being communicated.

The BrainPath model states that if you want people to be influenced by what you are presenting, then you must use stories that sequentially answer the questions that are happening in each section of their triune brains.

- Do I trust you? (Reptilian brain)
- Am I participating with you? (Limbic system)
- Have I experienced an 'Aha!' through you? (Cortex)

These three components make up the triune brain, each brain still present and affecting the way we make decisions. We will discuss how to create 'Aha!' through the use of parables in chapter nine (How to write and deliver business parables).

HOW TO GET YOUR CLIENTS TO 'AHA!'

Getting your clients to 'Aha!' is a process of mapping stories and parables to the brain's natural path of least resistance. This process, also known as 'traveling the BrainPath', is when you use parable points to communicate to people's emotional and logical brains, establish trust, encourage participation, and deliver the feeling of *'Aha!'*

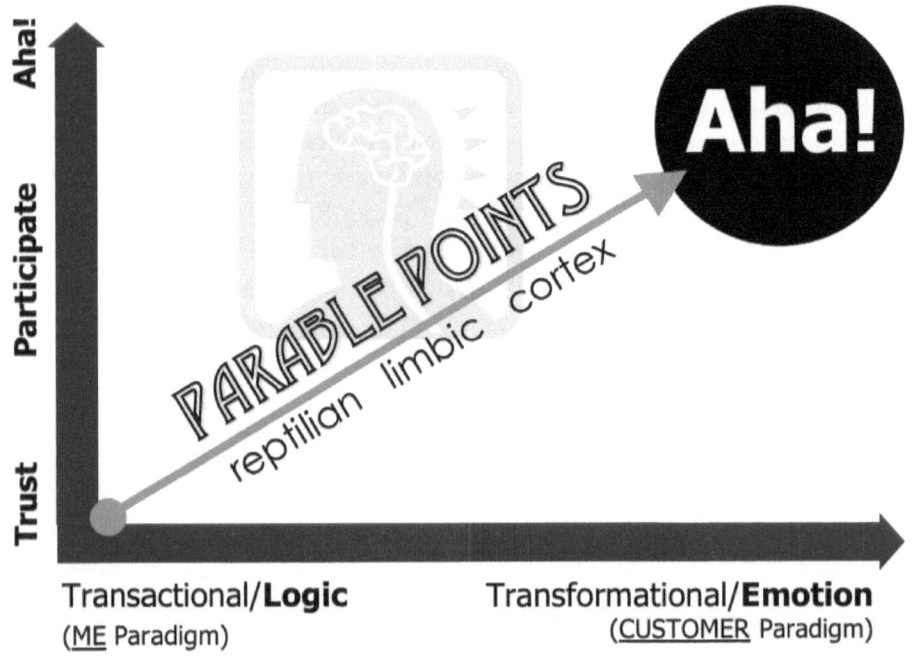

Figure 7.4. BrainPath: Getting Your Clients To 'Aha!'

Figure 7.4 represents the BrainPath process. First of all, notice that the sweet-spot, which is at the top right hand corner of the diagram, is when they reach 'Aha!' and say 'Yes!' – the ultimate goal of your business presentations.

Now let's go through the diagram in greater detail. Look at the 'x' and 'y' axes. The x-axis represents your leadership and discussion approach, which can range from transactional to transformational. It also represents the two extremes in the way you choose to communicate, either from a 'ME' paradigm, or a 'CUSTOMER' paradigm. Finally, the x-axis represents the two extremes in the way a listener processes the information you communicate to them. At one end is the logical or left-brain approach to cognition, while on the other end is the more emotional, right brain approach. Your task as a persuasive business presenter is to deliver your information more toward the right side of the continuum, in such a manner that your audience will perceive it with maximum emotional impact.

The y-axis represents your ability to address the three requirements for traversing the brain's information-handling process. First you must gain trust, (reptilian brain), then you must get audience members to participate, (limbic system), and finally, they must reach an "aha" (cortex), before a favorable decision can be made. The following table shows how all these various approaches come together in business presentations under the BrainPath model.

BrainPath	Reptilian	Limbic	Cortex
Presentation section	Beginning	Middle	End
Customer should Experience	Trust	Participation	*'Aha!'*
How its done	Get audience's ATTENTION within the first few minutes. Create TRUST in their minds about you and your company.	Deliver parable points about your benefits, and ask questions to get stories from them.	Help audiences discover their own *'Aha!'* moments. Ask for a specific ACTION, and turn them into inspired 'DISCIPLES' for your offering.
Aristotle's Rhetoric Model	Ethos (Credibility)	Logos (Logic)	Pathos (Emotions)

Most people start out in their business careers giving transactional, logic-based presentations, which can sometimes be incredibly boring. As you improve your ability to connect with listeners, your presentations become more effective and less dull. Nonetheless, many people reach the point where they are marginally effective, and then they become hijacked by their own prevailing business paradigms. If your communication style is dominated by the 'ME' paradigm, then you will be dragged back, time and again to boring, ineffective presentations. However, if your business paradigm is 100% about your customer, then you will address their needs, and quickly become an inspirational and persuasive business presenter. You will find it much easier to hit the sweet spot of 'Aha!' when you have mastered parable points – and are able to reach past the doubting logical mind, and into customers' emotions – where a favorable decision and inspired action can occur.

CASE STUDY

ANOTHER PARABLE OF 'HOW'

Early in my career, I sold manufacturing prospects on an enterprise software capability called Product Lifecycle Management (PLM), but the prospects just couldn't understand our value proposition. If you are involved in large companies that sell complex, technical products and services, you probably know the pattern: the sales people are usually on their own to create appropriate message for specific clients, and the general tendency is to pack the presentations with technical information and let the clients figure it out. We tried everything; demos, pilot installs, you name it – but nothing was getting through. Eventually, we exhausted all the fancy graphics and bullet-point slides our company had in its arsenal, and I decided to take the parable point approach, and created the following Parable:

turbulence...

:a state of disorder and disturbance

"A long time ago, pilots had to navigate manually through turbulence. Whenever there was a trouble-spot, they would grab the controls and pray for the best ...

Your enterprise experiences a similar discontinuity, friction, and 'turbulence' of information between applications, technologies, collaborators etc., costing you valuable time and money.

But did you know that there is a new invention that just surfaced, which can allow a pilot to intelligently anticipate turbulence points along the way and avoid them?

Think of PLM as a system that works this way, helping you facilitate the smooth, effortless flow of product information across your entire manufacturing lifecycle. Imagine the savings in money and time, the increase in data re-use and collaboration with suppliers, partners and even end-customers ... " – The clients finally got it ... it *worked*!

CHAPTER 4 SUMMARY

THE BRAIN'S SECRET PATH TO 'AHA!'

- Perception management is the process of getting your clients to experience 'Aha!'

- When selling complex concepts, you must dress up your facts, truth, and technical data in parables and stories to make your points more palatable for your audiences.

- Aristotle's ethos, pathos, and logos still holds true today...but advances in science now show us how to implement his theories along the BrainPath – the brain's path of least resistance to influence.

- Audiences must trust you, participate with you, and reach the breakthrough moment of clarity and understanding – 'Aha!'

- Getting your clients to 'YES' is achieved by arranging your parables and points along the BrainPath – which means organizing your presentation so that it is customer-focused, transformational, emotional, and achieves trust, participation, and 'Aha!'

EXERCISE

Review your current go-to-market presentation: Are you involving all three of Aristotle's recommendations for persuasive rhetoric?

- Ethos/Trust, Pathos/Participation, and Logos/'Aha!'?

Is your message successfully traveling up the BrainPath or is it getting stuck along the way?

5. The BrainPath™ StoryBoard Template

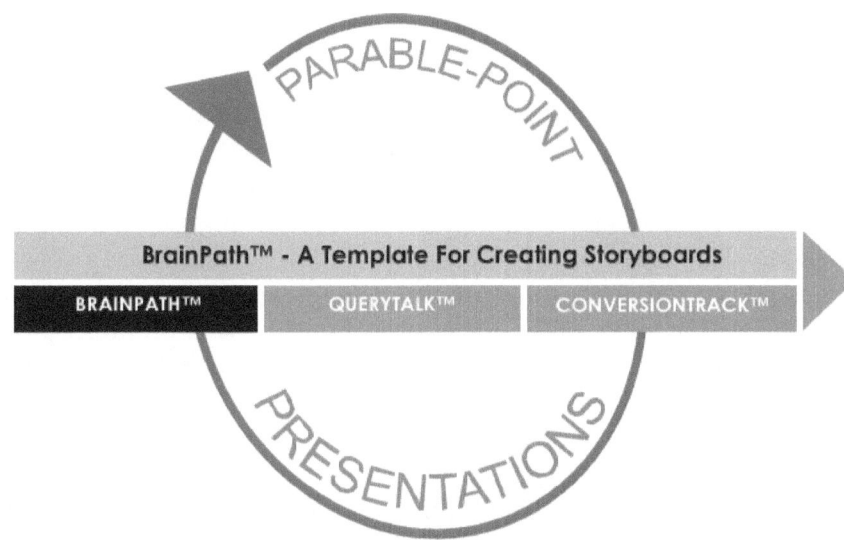

"Telling a story is such an artful way to instruct because it is so disarming; the tale seems to be about someone else, and yet the mind automatically draws the parallels to one's own life."
                              - DANIEL GOLEMAN

Are you ready to undergo a paradigm shift in the way you create and deliver business presentations? Are you ready to focus more on crafting emotional audience experiences for your clients than on conveying one-way, complex data and information? Are you ready to start winning more clients through business presentations? Congratulations! In this chapter, you will learn to do precisely that.

So far, we have discussed the human factors that affect business presentations. We have covered how you must *think* about business presentations before you can *do* them persuasively. Now it is time to bring these concepts all together within a system that will allow you to stand out from your competition on the business presentation platform. With the BrainPath™ template, you will be able to create powerful parable point presentations that focus more on your client's needs, and less on the natural, inadvertent 'ME' paradigm that so many people present from.

GUIDING PRINCIPLES

First, let us review the business presentation continuum we discussed in chapter 1, which shows the guiding principles that led to the parable point presentation system. Remember, your goal is to move away from ineffective bullet-points, and closer to transformational, interactive storytelling. The first order of business is that you recognize that the business presentation phase of any sales campaign is arguably the most mission-critical of all. You do not want to bore clients with bullet-points. Instead, you want to inspire them with *parable points*. Here are the guiding principles we have covered so far:

	Least effective		Most effective
	BULLET-POINTS	**BENEFIT-POINTS**	**PARABLE-POINTS™**
Style	Unidirectional	Transactional	Cognitive
Effect	Inform	Persuade	Inspire
Approach	Features	Benefits	Diagnose Client Needs
Focus	'ME'	Product	Customer
Message	'Push'	'Push'	'Pull'

Figure 5.1. The Business Presentation Continuum

1. **Style**: Clients don't respond well to unidirectional, transactional data being pushed at them, regardless of its relevance, and even if you demonstrate a good grasp of their business from your prior research. Your goal is to communicate along a *cognitive* path – the brain's path of least resistance to influence – so that your clients understand your information, remember it, and are influenced by it.

2. **Effect**: Information alone is not persuasive, and overt persuasion is very ineffective. Clients are more *inspired* when you build trust, encourage participation and lead them interactively toward an 'Aha!' experience.

3. **Approach**: Slides and bullet-points presented exclusively about your features and benefits are boring. Despite your prior research, you should not assume that you already know everything your client needs. Give them a chance to get involved during the presentation. Your goal is to ask questions and diagnose needs as an integral part of the process.

4. **Focus**: Clients want to know 'what's in it for them', or in other words, why they should buy your product or service. Speaking from a 'CUSTOMER' perspective is much more powerful than talking exclusively about you, your products, or your company.

5. **Message**: Clients, like all human beings, respond to stories better than to raw facts and data, which tend to feel force-fed. Stories, interactive activities, and exercises are *indirect*, and will 'pull' your listeners much more gently toward your point of view.

Remember that we talked earlier about the problem of presenting from a 'ME' point of view, and how that can really hurt your process of getting important points across? Well, there is really no other solution for talking about your client more or addressing their needs more unless you begin to present from an entirely different point of view; *their* point of view!

The **BrainPath**™ template is a multidimensional tool for creating storyboards that forces you to stop presenting in terms of YOUR solutions and YOUR benefits etc., which clients are naturally resistant to. Instead, you present based on how your CLIENT most optimally understands and accepts information. You learn to present along the **brain's path of least resistance!**

For most professionals, creating a presentation involves first firing up a software tool such as Microsoft's PowerPoint®, and then laying out bullet-points over a series of slides. This can lead to an over-reliance on the presentation software. In the parable point presentation system, your presentation software becomes a *second* step that comes only after you have completely brainstormed and designed an emotional audience experience. Here is the typical layout for most of today's bullet-point presentations – the sort that usually results in 'death by PowerPoint®':

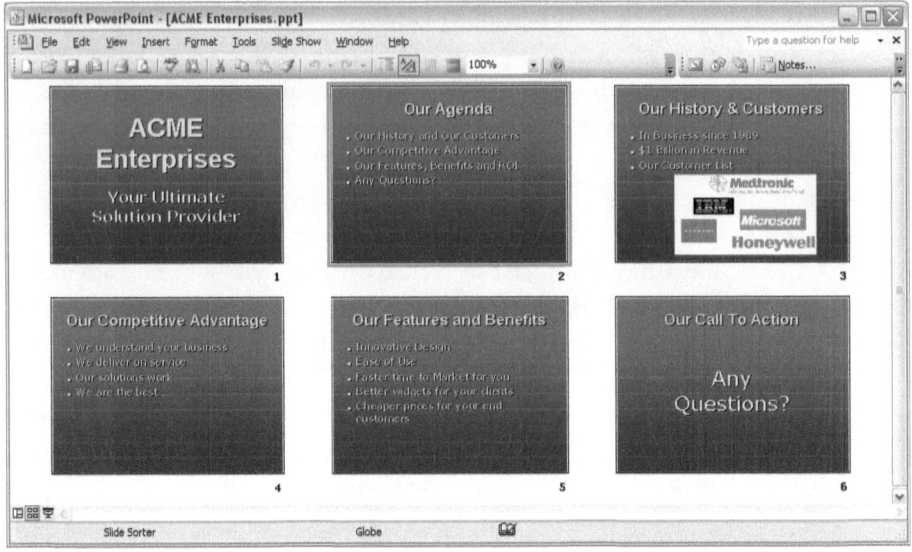

Figure 5.2. Typical Bullet-Point Layout for Most Presentations

Notice the heavy emphasis on 'our' in all these slides? Also, notice that most presentations leave audience questions for the end. This might work in many situations, but it is also a signal to your audience that you don't really want them participating, and that the stage is exclusively yours. Don't do that! The stage should also be *theirs*! Get them involved. Allow them to feel free to ask questions and participate, because through that interaction, trust is built, your credibility is established, and they become much more emotionally involved in whatever you're selling. The parable point approach takes you away from the 'ME-centric', non-interactive, bullet-point approach – and places you in closer proximity to your audience's emotions.

A 3-STEP PROCESS FOR CREATING PRESENTATIONS

The ultimate goal of your business presentation is to create an emotional *'Aha!'* experience in the minds of your listeners. We have discussed the fact that this *'Aha!'* experience is the key for influencing clients to ultimately make decisions in your favor. We have also reviewed the idea that this *'Aha!'* experience does not occur as a result of you speaking alone, and it certainly doesn't occur by listeners following bullet-points as you read them off. Rather, it takes both you and your listeners participating and telling stories for the perception gap to close, and for the emotional connection to occur. The parable point presentation system helps you reach your clients' emotions through storytelling and storylistening, brain-based adult learning techniques, and the art and science of influence.

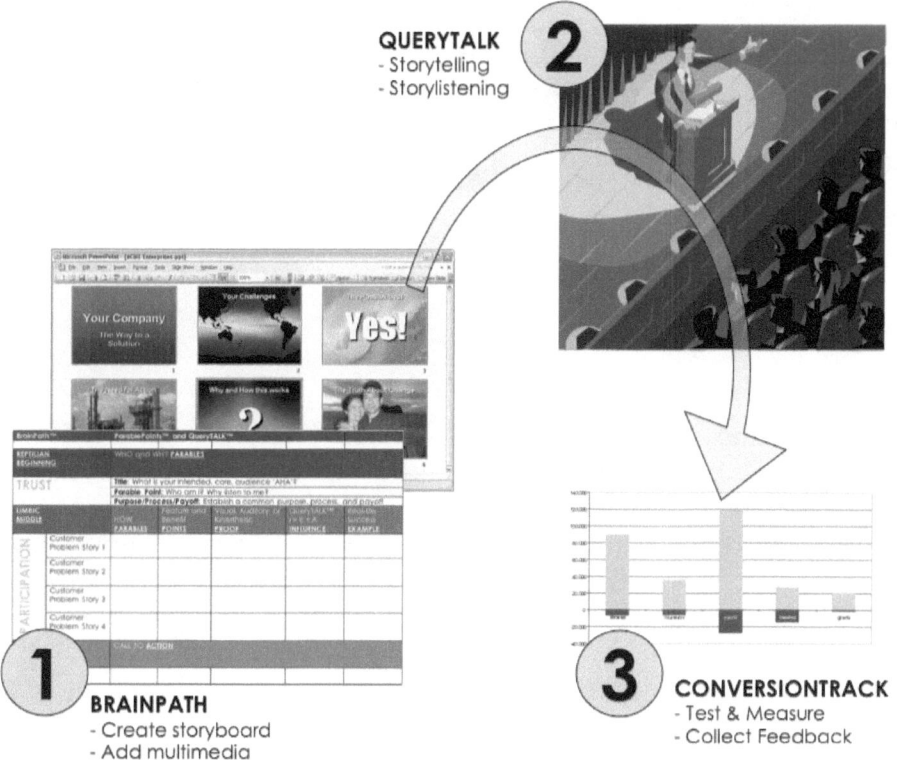

Figure 5.3. The three strategies of the parable point presentation system

Step 1: Create a Storyboard: The first step is to create a BrainPath™ storyboard – which serves as the overall plan or blueprint for your business presentation. The more detailed you are about planning your content and performance, the easier and more effective the presentation itself will be. When it comes to your overall messaging, you have to first get it right, then you have to tell it right, and then you have to measure your performance.

Step 2: Plan Your Delivery: The second step is to plan your performance by developing questions and methods for getting your audience to participate. This process of storytelling and storylistening is called QueryTalk.

Step 3: Prepare to Test and Measure: The last step is to put a specific system in place for practicing, perfecting, and then testing and measuring your presentations. Figure 5.3 shows how these three strategies work together as part of a parable point presentation process.

> Your core task is to inspire people to action by replacing bullet-points with parable points; raw data with stories; and complexity with emotional, persuasive engagement.

Imagine that you have been asked to give a one-hour, mission-critical presentation to a prospect, and you will have anywhere from five to fifteen people in attendance, including the decision-maker. Your task in this presentation is to introduce your product, which has complex features and benefits, and which the audience is not very familiar with. How will you begin? Will you pull out a generic presentation and update it to fit this new audience? Will you start by listing out your entire product's features and how they deliver customer benefits? Or will you start by writing down all the points that differentiate your company from the competition? If these are your starting points, then, like a majority of people in the business world, you have already made a critical mistake! You are in danger of starting with a 'ME' paradigm!

The parable point presentation system calls for a different approach – as Stephen Covey once wrote, "Start with the end in mind." Think in terms of what the 'CUSTOMER' wants to achieve by asking yourself:

"What are my customer's challenges and desired outcomes?"

"What is the core audience 'Aha!' that I want my listeners to experience in relation to those challenges and desired outcomes?"

"What will be my "Call to Action?"

Once you know what the end should be, then you must return to brainstorming all the features and benefits that your product or service provides, and then create parables that will help you better explain them. Overall, you must do everything in the language of your audience's interests, not yours, and you must bypass their logical, doubting minds, and speak directly to their emotions. The best way to do this is with stories, and the parable point storyboard template (Figure 8.6) will guide you through the process of creating them.

> The basic premise of the parable point presentation system is that influence cannot be achieved in the absence of active participation from your audience.
>
> You are the guide, helping them experience *'Aha!'* Their solution is already within them, and instead of being a torchlight shining brightly in their faces, you must become a lighthouse – an assurance of safety in the distance. You must try to enroll, not convince; pull instead of push; for your audience will find you through stories and participation.

THE STRUCTURE OF A BRAINPATH™ STORYBOARD

Imagine if your audience could tell you exactly what would inspire and influence them, and in what order you should provide these things to them! If that were the case, you would have a perfect, persuasive, and inspirational presentation each time! Remember our age-old wisdom from chapter 1?

> *Give a man a fish, and feed him for a day;*
> *Teach him how to fish and feed him for a lifetime;*
> *But teach him how to think like a fish, and he'll feed himself and his village*
> *for generations.*

Well, if clients were fish, and you wanted to catch lots of them, you must learn to *think* like them. While we can do a reasonably good job of imagining what clients are thinking during business presentations, human nature usually gets in the way, and we revert back to our old one-way presentation habits. Since it is not possible to know exactly what clients think at all times, we can reliably look to neuroscience to give us a close approximation of what happens in people's minds during presentations, and what it will therefore take to influence them. The bottom line is this: the best way to communicate in a business presentation is along the BrainPath - the path of least resistance for your message.

In chapter four (The Brain's Secret Path to 'Aha!'), we discussed the brain's triune configuration, which has evolved over time. We reviewed how signals that come into the eyes and ears first go through the reptilian brain, (specifically, the amygdala), and are then routed to the limbic system and eventually, the cortex. We discussed the different specializations for each of these "three brains", and how an audience must experience a "whole-brained" experience in order for true learning and inspiration to occur. We also have reviewed the power inherent in simple stories: how parables can transport a listener to a place of metaphor, where they can more safely (and indirectly) get answers to the questions that are burning in their minds. We have also discussed the fact that audience participation leads to better idea retention and allows them to transfer your information into new and different circumstances. Finally, we discussed how parables, bite-sized stories with powerful messages, have the ability to achieve these various objectives. Now let us review what is really happening in your audience members' minds during your presentation, bearing in mind that if you do not address these needs, their minds will 'shut off' and they will tune you out, and start looking at their watches!

> The **BrainPath** is the path of least resistance by which the brain accepts new information. It is the best way the brain will learn, remember, and be influenced by what you present.

Figure 5.4 shows how the brain constantly processes information and waits to receive specific assurances at each stage of a presentation. To remain fully engaged with what you are saying, the audience needs answers to the following questions:

1. First, the *reptilian* brain asks: "Can I **trust** you?"

2. Then throughout the presentation, the *limbic* brain asks: "Am I **participating**?"

3. Toward the end, the *cortex* brain asks: "When will I experience an '**aha**'?"

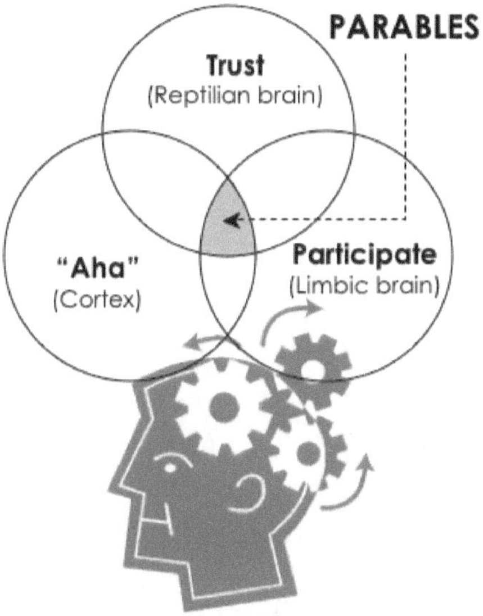

Figure 5.4. The BrainPath approach to designing presentations

The questions in the listening brain therefore form the order and main objectives for the *timeline* of your entire presentation: (a) create trust, (b) encourage participation, and (c) produce *'Aha!'*

Figure \5.5 shows the two axes of the BrainPath template. The arrow on the left pointing down represents your presentation's overall *timeline*, which is divided into three sections. These sections also map to a clear beginning, middle, and end for your presentation, which is congruent with Aristotle's universal description of good story structure. The arrow on the top pointing right represents the actual *content* of each section. This template will guide you to create all the headlines and parable points that you will eventually use for creating your presentation, and later, you will export these ideas into whatever presentation software system you will use for added multimedia effect.

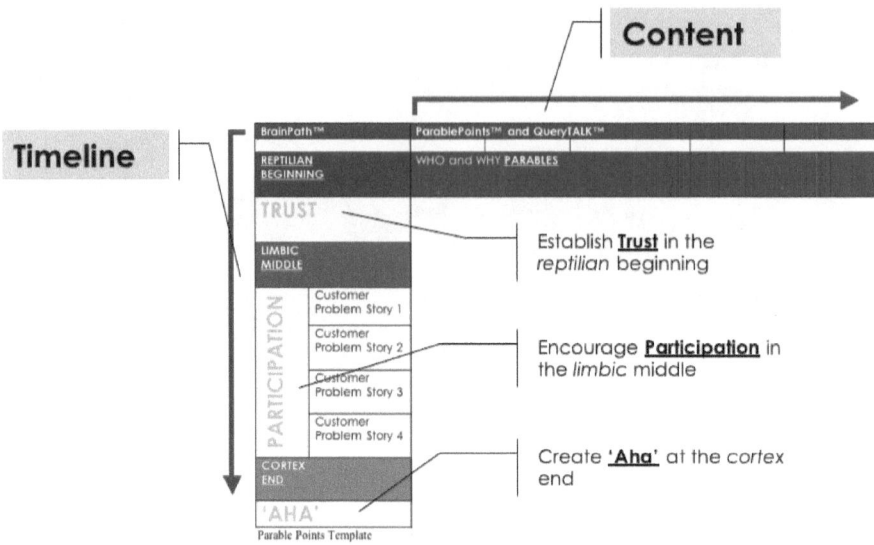

Figure 5.5. The BrainPath Storyboard Axes: Timeline and Content

Notice the headings of the various sections of the BrainPath template on the following page. (Figure 5.6) In the BrainPath template, the beginning, middle, and end are represented by the brain's need for trust, participation, and aha respectively. Thus the three sections of the BrainPath storyboard template are called, the reptilian beginning, the limbic middle, and the cortex end.

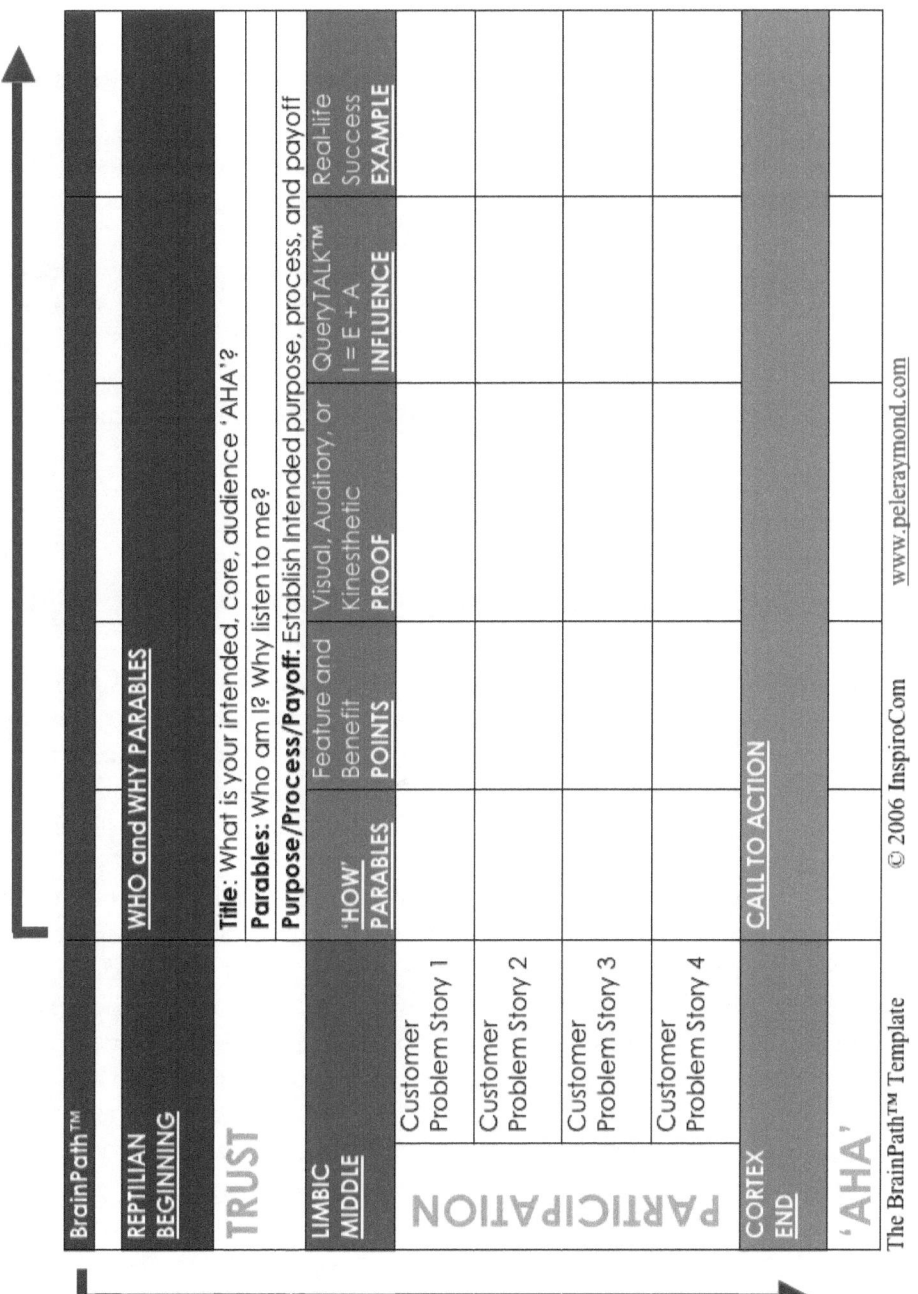

Figure 5.6. The BrainPath Storyboard Template

THE FOUR STEPS FOR CREATING A BRAINPATH STORYBOARD

There are four steps required for creating a storyboard using the BrainPath storyboard template:

1. Reptilian Beginning (Create the section that will earn trust).
2. Limbic Middle (Encourage participation while conveying your parables and points).
3. Cortex 'Aha!' (Deliver the 'Aha'! and Call to Action).
4. Multimedia (Add the images and audio that will accompany your presentation).

Let us review each stage in more detail.

1. The Reptilian <u>Beginning</u> (Earn Trust)

In chapter three, (Its About Connecting, Not Public Speaking), I gave the example of the day I had to turn off lights in a presentation so that my audience could see the visuals better. Noticing that the audience was at first uneasy, I disarmed them with self-deprecating humor. I had to first get them comfortable with me before I could proceed to sharing a meaningful experience with them.

The first two or three minutes of your presentation represent the only chance you'll have to earn the audience's attention and trust, or else you'll lose it for good. From the minute you step onto the podium, the audience begins to judge you. They will look at your clothes, your grooming, and every possible detail of your appearance in order to make sense of the simple question that is playing in their heads: "Do we trust this person?" Once you begin talking, you shift their attention to what you are saying, and you now have an opportunity to alter any potential stereotypes or assumptions that may already be working against you. The most important thing your presentation must accomplish in the reptilian beginning is to create an emotional connection between you and the audience. To accomplish this, you must help them answer the following questions burning in their reptilian brains:

- Who are you?
- Why should we listen to you?
- What do you sell? A product, service, or an idea?
- What is in it for us if we listen to you?

REPTILIAN BEGINNING	WHO and WHY **PARABLES**
TRUST	**Title**: What is your intended, core, audience 'AHA'?
	Parable Point: Who am I? Why listen to me?
	Purpose/Process/Payoff: Establish a common purpose, process, and payoff

Figure 5.7. The Reptilian Beginning – answering the question of trust

Before you begin discussing your offering, or even your customer's problems, answer these questions for them, and make them feel safe. The best way to do this is to disarm the audience with questions or tell them a short parable. If you are confident comedian, you might want to try a humorous opening, but for most people, a well-planned introductory story is quite sufficient. (The parable of "who" you are). Consider your audience; are they going to be receptive to a well-placed joke? If they are a very technical group, maybe you can lead with a small exercise instead that gets them to participate right up front. Whatever you do in the reptilian beginning, remember that your objective is simply to catch their attention and earn the right to tell them who you are and why they should listen to you. Here's an example from one of my favorite speakers. World-renowned motivational speaker Les Brown never starts a speech, until he encourages participation and has told his parable of 'who' he is, and where he's from. He usually starts out with something like this:

"Hello, I'm Les Brown. How many of you here have important goals you want to achieve?" [Hands get raised in the audience…participation begins].

"Well I'm here to tell you that it's possible!

For example, I never knew that I could become what I am today! I never knew that, as a child, born with my twin brother in Liberty city, abandoned on a floor, given up for dead … I never knew that I had what it took to become the success I am today. I never knew …"

Les Brown's parable accomplishes two things; first, he establishes credibility – he is a success today, and look how far he traveled to get here. He is also giving you a sense of perspective about his history, thus preparing you for his core message, which is this: if he can do it, so can you.

> Create your own reptilian beginning parable, try it out on different audiences, and develop the best one for your trade and style.

The final thing you want to accomplish in the reptilian beginning is to invite the audience to participate with you in your presentation. You do this by laying down some rules:

1. **Purpose**: First, you will explain why this presentation is needed today.
2. **Process**: Next, you will explain what you want them to do during the presentation. (i.e., you will invite them to share their own experiences along the way)
3. **Payoff**: Finally, you will tell them what they are going to gain from this presentation.

These three points will conclude your reptilian beginning section. You have now answered the questions of who you are, why you're here, why they should listen to you, and what the process for today's discussion will be. You are now ready to get into the main presentation itself. Do not underestimate the importance of this reptilian beginning process. Remember that we are emotional beings first, and our guard is always up when we first meet strangers. Evolution and survival have predisposed human beings to see negatives before positives, so you have to seize your audience's attention and quickly frame the discussion toward a positive experience.

2. The Limbic <u>Middle</u> (Encourage Participation)

Now you are ready to begin going through a list of benefit points that address customer problems. It is important to adhere to the following steps for populating each 'customer problem story'. (Figure 5.8)

LIMBIC MIDDLE		'HOW' PARABLES	Feature and Benefit POINTS	Visual, Auditory, or Kinesthetic PROOF	QueryTALK™ I = E + A INFLUENCE	Real-life Success EXAMPLE
PARTICIPATION	Customer Problem Story 1					
	Customer Problem Story 2					
	Customer Problem Story 3					
	Customer Problem Story 4					

Figure 5.8. The Limbic Middle – establishing customer benefit points

1. **Customer Problem**: Based on your prior research, identify a customer problem that your product or service addresses. Name each thread based on the client's challenges or needs, not your product's features or capabilities.
2. **Parable of How**: Create a parable, metaphor, or analogy for how the feature actually works and provides a benefit to your clients. This parable must also get their attention, and get them thinking.
3. **Benefit Point**: State the point of the parable you just presented.
4. **Proof**: Provide evidence of how your client might experience proof that this feature actually works.
5. **Influence**: Involve the audience by asking questions in accordance with the laws of influence (I = E + A).
6. **Examples**: Provide at least one real-life example to further illustrate how others have experienced this benefit.

Now repeat steps one through six for each of the customer problems you've identified. This way, you go through all of the customer's challenges that your presentation will address. In each step, you are systematically getting their attention with a parable, clarifying exactly what benefit you're providing, giving the examples and proof that it really works, and using the rules of influence and participation throughout.

3. The Cortex <u>End</u> (Deliver *'Aha!'* and Call to Action)

Now that you have completed the main portion of the presentation, it is time to summarize and state your call to action. At this point, the client knows who you are, trusts you, has shared stories with you, and has received both factual and emotional reasons to buy your product. Now its time for the coup de grace – delivering the *'Aha!'*

CORTEX END	CALL TO ACTION				
'AHA'					

Figure 5.9. The Cortex End – delivering the *'Aha!'* and a call to action

The purpose of this last phase of your presentation is to summarize by restating the main benefit points that you presented during the limbic middle. Remind the listeners of the parables and points you used to get their attention, and restate the points made and how they provide real benefits. Now give them a final parable, metaphor, or analogy that concludes and leaves them with the most important 'Aha!' of all – something they will remember, and hopefully repeat to others in your absence.

Now that you have made all of your competitive advantages clear to the audience, you need to ask for something. Ask them to take a specific action in favor of your campaign. This is arguably the most critical part of your presentation, because if you don't call them to action – *ask for something* – then all you have done so far is provide entertainment. State clearly what actions you want your listeners to take as a result of all the things that you have presented so far. These actions don't have to be 'buy the product now!' – you may simply want to encourage them to move to the next phase of their buying process. Regardless of what you ask for, don't make it open-ended. The response you want from them should be either 'yes' or 'no'. There should be no room for a 'maybe' response, or else you have wasted their time and yours. Get bold. Ask for the sale.

4. Adding Multimedia To The BrainPath

Now that you have designed the presentation in storyboard template form, you are ready to move your ideas into a multimedia software presentation program. (Such as Microsoft's PowerPoint®, or Apple's KeyNote). It is very important that this is a second step, because you'll avoid the temptation of building your presentation around your bullet-points and graphics, instead of the core messages that you want delivered.

There are essentially two ways you can view the use of multimedia in presentations. You can use the medium as a unidirectional data tool, or you can use it as a means of supporting a **cognitive influence** campaign. Here is the difference between the two approaches:

Unidirectional data	Cognitive influence
One-way data dump	The BrainPath guides your placement of messages and images
PowerPoint® is center stage	Speaker is center stage
Lots of Bullet-points	No Bullet-points
PowerPoint® can be read and understood as a handout	The presentation cannot be understood completely on its own without the speaker.
Pictures to support bullet-points	Pictures as a central tool for communicating emotion along with the words being spoken per slide.
Text dominates the slides – forcing audiences to read while you speak	Very limited use of text – single words used instead to get attention and add power to a point being spoken verbally.
Headlines are long and 'ME' focused	Headlines are short, catchy, and client-focused.

Figure 5.10 is an example of how a presentation's slides should look: more graphics, less bullet-points. Tell your audience the story, instead of forcing them to read bullet-points. For further reading on creating reduced-text multimedia, I recommend Cliff Atkinson's book published by Microsoft Press – *Beyond Bullet-points* – for a more thorough explanation of how to create PowerPoint® multimedia with little or no bullet-points (Atkinson, 2005).

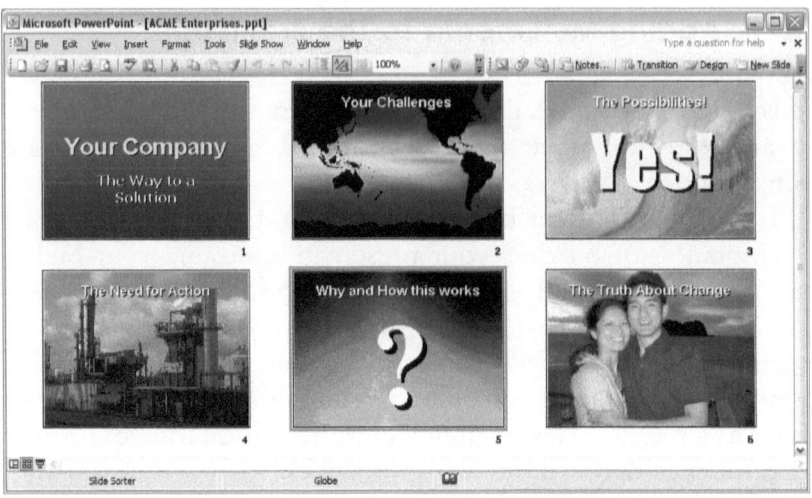

Figure 5.10. A 'No-bullet-points' Approach to Multimedia.

The best way to use PowerPoint® is in the context of a learning approach renowned psychology professor Dr. Richard Mayer calls *meaningful transfer*, which goes beyond what is known as mere *retention*. Retention is when people might remember what you presented, but transfer is when they not only remember it, but are able to apply the knowledge you provided to solve problems in new, different situations. The best way to promote meaningful transfer is through storytelling. This means that audiences will internalize what you say, and will use it to solve problems even when you are not around. Dr. Richard Mayer reveals that *participation* is an important and critical component for achieving the 'transfer' level of learning. Here is Dr. Mayer's finding on 'meaningful' learning:

> Retention is the ability to remember material at some later time in much the same way it was presented during instruction. Transfer is the ability to use what was learned to solve problems, answer questions, or facilitate learning new subject matter . . . Stated somewhat differently, retention focuses on the past; transfer emphasizes the future. (Mayer, 2002, Para 2)

"Transfer" is achieved through **storytelling**. A story is a narration of something that really happened. People will remember a story or parable much longer than facts and data.

In closing, remember that multimedia must always be used as a supporting prop, not as the main attraction. The main attraction must always be the speaker, and the actual content of her stories. Some good examples for the use of multimedia can be found in Al Gore's movie, *An Inconvenient Truth*, and also in Steve Jobs' keynotes delivered at Apple's annual MacWorld conference and expo in 2007. Both of these presentations were powerful, audience-focused, influential, and used little or no bullet-points. Both presentations are great examples of how to use multimedia to play an important, yet supporting role in a business presentation.

THE BRAINPATH TEMPLATE

The following is a set of questions that you can answer as part of creating your parable point presentation;

- What are the major customer-challenge 'Ahas' that I want to communicate? Are they things my customer will care about? What is my ultimate, intended call to action?

- How am I going to establish trust in the first few minutes of this presentation? Will I use a parable, some audience interaction, or a joke?

- Now that I am about to enter into the 'body' of the presentation, how will I encourage my audience to participate as we go along? How can I get them to share their stories with me? What specific questions will I ask?

- What specific points will I make, and which parables of *how my solution works* will I use?

- Will I ask lots of questions and dig deeper when someone responds? How will I magnify their emotions?

- Now that I have made my major points, and we have interacted, it is time for my final summary and 'Aha!' What parable or story will I use to make my last, poignant point?

SOLUTION **2** : QUERYTALK

The 3 Big Mistakes	The 3 Big Solutions
1. The '**ME**' Mindset	BrainPath™ Storyboarding
2. One-Way **bullet-point** slides	QueryTalk™ Storytelling
3. No **system** for improvement	ConversionTrack™

In order to win more clients, you need a systematic process for delivering persuasive presentations that are reliable, repeatable, and are based on scientific evidence. In solution 2, you will learn how to deliver business presentations through QueryTalk™:

- Dynamic speaking in is not required for winning more clients; but emotional connection is.
- There is a large body of scientific research that shows the clear principles by which people are influenced.
- The ancient art of storytelling is at the center of any attempt to verbally influence clients in business presentations.
- You will learn to create your own business parables, especially the parables of *Who*, *Why*, and *How*.
- How to use the QueryTalk™ template to create your presentation content.

In solution 1, we explored the mindset you need and the method for designing persuasive business presentations. The following chapters in Solution 2 will cover the science behind the system, and show you how to deliver your parable point presentations.

6. It's About Connecting, Not Just Speaking

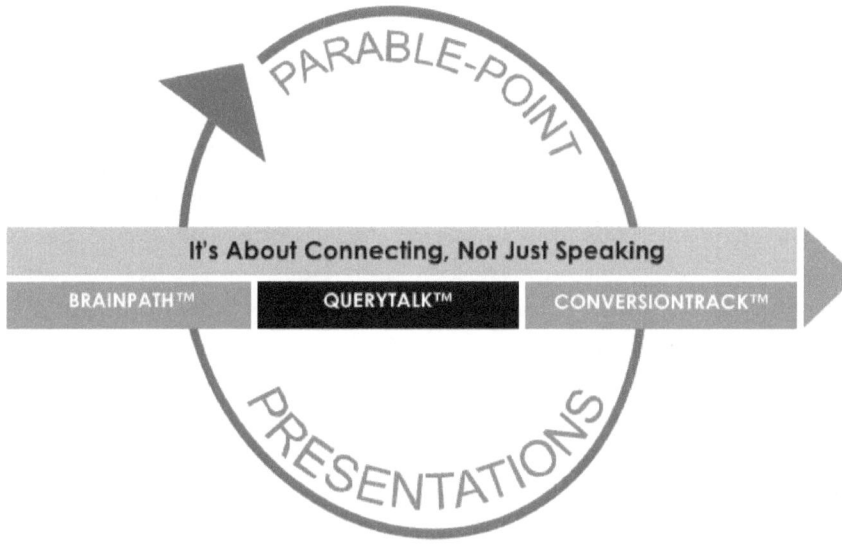

"It is a myth, not a mandate, a fable, not a logic, and a symbol rather than a reason by which men are moved."
                                                    - IRWIN EDMAN

The jet-black man in a dark, ebony-colored suit entered the rear of the conference room and surveyed the crowd. As he walked slowly toward the front of the room, the audience studied him in return, with a hint of mild and increasing anxiety. In order to maximize the visual quality of the presentation images beamed on the overheads, he began turning off the lights as he approached the podium. An associate of his on the other side of the room similarly turned off other lights. Some audience members began looking around anxiously, as though in search of the closest exits. As he finally gained the podium, he yelled to his confederate: "Hey, leave that last one on! If you turn off that light, these poor folks will only be able to see my eyes and my teeth!" The audience erupted into a welcome laughter, which cut through the tension like a knife. A crucial *emotional* connection had just been made, and the outcome of that presentation was a client purchase worth millions of dollars.

I was the jet-black man, and that was one of many influential business presentations I gave while selling complex software technology and services as a director of marketing in corporate America. The audience's reaction in the split second when they laughed had more to do with the success of that particular event than most people might realize. The actual, play-by-play biology behind that audience's instinctive reaction has only recently been revealed through cutting edge brain research, and yet, what happened in their brains is the result of an art form that is as ancient as humankind itself. Current science now illuminates ancient art, showing us that our decision-making brains have more to do with feelings and reflexes occurring at a primal level, than with what we see, hear, or know logically. By putting the audience at ease – making them feel safe – I went a long way toward earning the right to influence them. That silly joke did more than bullet-points could have done in an hour; it helped me earn from my audience the basic emotion of *trust*. Neuroscience is able to tell us definitively that, at a biological level, humans process information first through a set of basic emotions, before logic gets a chance to take hold (Ekman, 1992).

> What most people don't realize is that we are *feeling* beings who think, not *thinking* beings who feel. Think how much more effective you could be if your business presentations could **connect** directly and powerfully to people's feelings ... to the place in the mind where true decisions are made.

Have you ever wondered why so many business professionals find it hard to connect with their audiences? The answer lies in the beliefs, thought patterns, and the type of *mindset* with which they present. This chapter deals with three of the most common myths that are responsible for this challenge:

- Myth #1: Persuasion requires dynamic public speaking skills.
- Myth #2: All you need is PowerPoint® – so just wing it!
- Myth #3: Logic-based information is paramount.

Let us examine each myth in greater detail.

MYTH #1: PERSUASION REQUIRES DYNAMIC SPEAKING

This myth couldn't be further from the truth. Influence in business presentations is not about dynamism or flamboyance; it is about connection. From your client's point of view, the most important requirements for an influential experience are that they learn something, remember the points, and are able to apply the new knowledge in future (decision-making) situations (Mayer, 2002). None of these requirements are related to proficiency or dynamism in public speaking. Speaking well and appearing confident can certainly help, but that comes with preparation, practice, and knowing your subject well. Influence is totally different; it is achieved through magnetism, not dynamism. What you really need as a presenter is an ability to *connect emotionally* with your audience. When your audience is emotionally engaged, they will be more committed to your words.

> To achieve emotional connection with audiences, and thereby become more persuasive in business presentations, you must focus your mind on **storytelling** and asking **questions**, not *public speaking*.

So, how do you learn to tell business stories? Go back for a moment to grade school. Do you remember telling your friends stories during recess? Do you remember walking home with a friend, talking about events at school? Do you remember ever being at a camp somewhere, and sharing campfire stories about life with friends? All of these activities were done naturally, without any focus on 'how you sounded' or 'how you looked' while delivering these stories. No one taught you how to effectively tell stories – you did so naturally – and yet, these stories were effective in getting your point across to your 'public', and possibly even in persuading them to take some kind of action. You already know how to tell stories. You just need to bring that capability to business presentations. In order to influence people, you have to boil your presentations down to a series of stories. Speak naturally, and these stories will be a more effective tool than any 'dynamic' speech you could ever give.

Persuasion happens when people are emotionally able to 'step into your shoes', participate in shared experiences, and see the world from a different point of view. Getting people to that point involves several direct and indirect approaches, but the easiest of these is sharing stories. Research shows that when consumers are presented with an indirect metaphorical claim, they are much more receptive to the ideas being presented (McQuarrie & Phillips, 2005). A business story is essentially a way of making your claim through metaphor. People are moved by simple stories in a way that oratorical prowess and rhetoric can never match. When you tell stories, you have the unique quality of transporting people to a place outside of their own logical minds, doubts, and current reality − into a world that you control. Once people follow you to the 'place' created in your story, you can insert your points into that world, close the *value perception gap*, and your ideas will be much more easily accepted.

Every presentation begins with a perception gap, which is the difference between what you know, and what you eventually want your client to agree with. What you know and want is delivered through your stories, but you must also ask questions to get your client to tell you their stories. Through your client's stories, you will more clearly understand what they really want. Through this exchange, you will gain the keys to closing the perception gap. Be careful to note that these two goals − yours and theirs − may not be exactly congruent at the beginning of any presentation. You must ask and clarify *what the client expects and wants* and have that in the back of your head throughout the presentation.

When you start a typical presentation, you have some ideas you want to communicate, and a set of goals − the results that you want. Similarly, your client also has a set of stated or unstated goals and current understandings. Your goal is to use your stories as allegorical tools to challenge the stories already in their heads regarding the value of your offering. Your goal is also to ask the client strategic questions that will invite them to tell you some of their challenges − *their* stories. Sharing stories will bring the two sides closer together, and close the value perception gap. Figure 6.1 shows how a typical business presentation starts out.

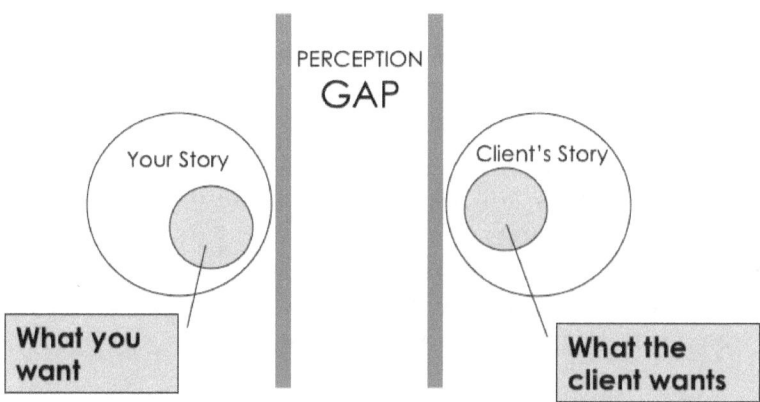

Figure 6.1. The Business Presentation 'Perception gap'

Figure 6.2 shows the next phase, which is what happens as you begin to tell stories and invite your audience members to do the same. The stories draw you and your listeners together, creating the crucial emotional connections that help you close the perception gap.

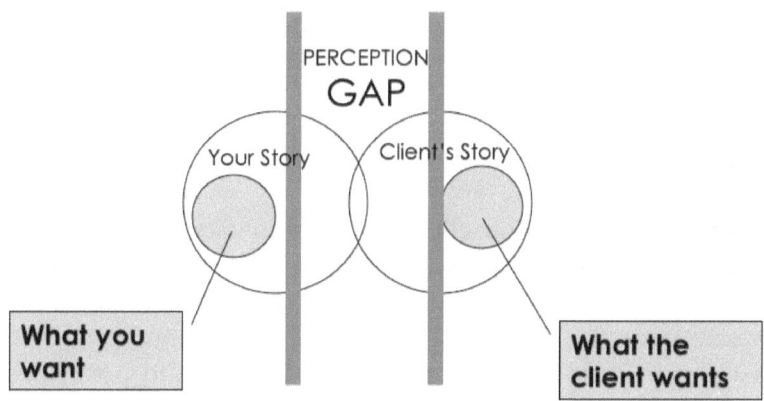

Figure 6.2. Closing the Business Presentation 'Perception gap'

A parable point presentation is designed around the process of connecting emotionally, so that you can close the perception gap. Instead of one-way communication performances, you meticulously plan a presentation that engages your audience bi-directionally, encouraging them to talk to you almost as much as you talk to them. Your ultimate goal for business presentations is to achieve a 'coming together' of stories. Your stories will challenge and influence the stories and objections your audience members may already have in their minds, while their stories will help you increase your empathy and understand their challenges. Both parties will be able to 'step into each other's shoes'. Ultimately, as seen in Figure 6.3, your goal is to eliminate the perception gap altogether, so that there is congruence between what you want, (which is to sell something), and what the client ultimately needs and wants (which is to buy the *right* solution).

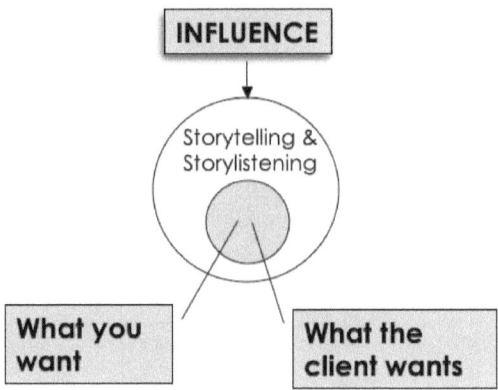

Figure 6.3. Influence: The Result of Connecting in Business Presentations

If you want to increase you client conversion rates, you must learn to *influence* prospects to see the world as you do, and your best tool is storytelling – a skill you have been preparing and polishing all your life. You already have the basics. All you need to do now is learn how to apply it to your business presentations. Your ability to persuade hinges on your ability to connect; and the best way to connect with people is through stories. Once you learn to replace the 'public speaking' mindset with storytelling and storylistening, you will be able to do away with any limiting fears you may harbor about public speaking, and become a better, more influential business presenter.

The concept of telling stories as a strategy for influence is critical, but it represents only half of the equation. The second part of any strategy for influence is in asking *Socratic* questions that encourage your listener to tell you *their* stories. Asking questions shows that you care, and as you are probably aware, people find it hard to care about your points unless they feel that you care about theirs. They see you as *interesting* only when they feel you are *interested* in them. You will gain much more influence in a session of question-asking than in a speech loaded with information-telling.

The Socratic method is derived from the ancient *Socratic Dialogues* of Plato, in which Socrates was said to have made his listeners arrive at conclusions they ordinarily wouldn't have thought of through the simple power of asking questions. Although Socrates used this method of asking questions for an adversarial purpose, (for example, he used it to humiliate or even demoralize his respondents), when used respectfully, it is a very effective method for gaining agreement or understanding from skeptical listeners. Here is an example of how I once used a parable and the Socratic method to explain the concept of 'chunking' in a business-coaching situation with a client:

Me: "Getting your business planned and started is similar to an elephant that you have to eat all by yourself. It can be overwhelming. Let me share with you the Parable of the Elephant. Imagine if we brought an elephant into the room here, and asked you to eat it. What would be your strategy?"

Client: "I would start from whatever body part was nearest to me, and start chewing. You have to start from somewhere."

Me: "That's right. But what if it kicked you in the head?"

Client: "Oh, I get it. You're saying it's still alive. Okay, I guess I'd have to kill it first."

Me: "That's right. What tools would you use?"

Client: "I guess I'd have to get a gun to kill it, and a knife and fork to eat it."

Me: "That's right. What would you do with the knife?"

Client: "I'd cut the elephant up into individual little pieces I could swallow at a time."

Me: "That's right. And that's how you should handle your business. Don't focus on how daunting your plan is, or in this parable, how big the elephant is. First, analyze it, reduce it to small, more manageable *chunks*, and put yourself on a schedule to eat the entire elephant, one small bite at a time!"

The client immediately reached an 'Aha!' by answering those questions. This process of talking through questions is at the heart of the QueryTalk strategy. It is an invaluable way to both involve your audience, and get them to arrive at conclusions on their own. Remember, people believe what they figure out on their own, or say themselves, much more than whatever we can tell them. Asking questions is much more powerful than telling people things, and you certainly don't need to be a dynamic speaker to ask questions.

MYTH #2: ALL YOU NEED IS POWERPOINT® – SO WING IT!

One of the biggest problems with business presentations is an over-reliance on PowerPoint®. Many have gained comfort in front of software slideshows – a technology that is so useful and straightforward that most people have formed the impression that no training is needed in order to use it for important presentations. The predominant belief in business presentations today is that "all you need is PowerPoint®," and that you can just fire up a slideshow, and essentially 'wing-it', or 'fake-it-till-you-make-it'. What happens is that the real challenge – effective, influential communication with clients – is conveniently avoided, and what is left is a process of boiling issues down into lists, where they lose their persuasive power in a litany of bullet-points and text.

The result of this dependence on PowerPoint® is the pervasiveness of mediocrity and 'unconscious incompetence' when it comes to business presenting – in other words, people don't know that they don't know what they don't know. They are unaware of the amount of careful preparation and planning that experienced presenters put into mastering the business presentation medium, and making it appear effortless. They are unaware of how much more influential they could be if they turned the PowerPoint® slides off – and simply conversed with their prospects.

Professor Todd Parker of DePaul University summarized this problem quite well:

"My biggest complaint is that [the slides] come between the teacher and his or her students. The danger is that class tends to devolve into a slide show from which students too often retreat to that room behind their eyeballs. My seven years at DePaul have taught me that the most valuable relationship between teacher and student is charismatic and immediate, one in which the teacher actively engages the students personally. This is hard to do when you turn the effort of instruction over to a machine." - Goodman (2005)

If your goal is to persuade audiences to take action, then you need to realize that there is a lot more to a business presentation than just loading up slides and putting bullet-points up on a board. There is an entire science behind how people listen, understand, and remember – all critical results that you need from each of your presentations – and it has very little to do with bullet-points. In order to be very effective at presenting, you need to know the science – the *how* and *why* – behind audience behavior both during and after a meeting. If you understand how and why certain strategies work, you'll be better equipped to perform successfully in different situations. You will quickly develop to a state of mastery, conscious competence, and seemingly effortless presentations. The objective of this book is to facilitate that process.

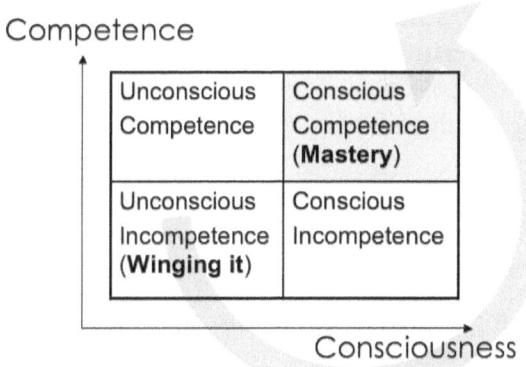

Figure 6.4. From 'Winging It' to Mastery and Conscious Competence.

Figure 6.4 is a way of showing the progression from unconscious to conscious competence. First, in the bottom-left quadrant, you have people who 'don't know that they don't know'. This means that they watch others present, and when the time comes, they simply fire up their own PowerPoint® slides and start reading the bullet-points they see on the screen. These kinds of presenters are simply not aware of the damage they are doing to the business points they are trying to communicate. The result of this approach is usually audiences who are busy wondering why you don't just give them a handout to take home – so they can read it for themselves!

Next, in the bottom-right quadrant – moving toward greater consciousness – are those people who have begun to recognize that there are methods and technologies they could learn to improve their persuasiveness and effectiveness. Such people begin to actively seek new knowledge and methods to improve their skills. They are consciously incompetent, and have come to the place in their minds where they are ready to learn what they don't know, so they can fix it, and move to the next stage of conscious competence.

In the top-right quadrant, moving upwards toward more competence, are those who are competent, and conscious of it. This is the most desirable state, which is when you know *exactly* what you are doing and why it gets the results you desire. Your ultimate goal is to move toward this conscious competence – the state of mastery in which you know exactly what effects you are having on the minds and emotions of your listeners. Over time, you will go beyond this stage, and reach a point in which you persuade naturally, using all the methods you have acquired over time. At this stage, (unconscious competence), you are now so good that you don't even have to think about it.

MYTH #3: LOGIC-BASED INFORMATION IS PARAMOUNT

Western societies are culturally hardwired and taught to deliver business information using logic, facts and data, instead of striving for emotional impact through storytelling. Most business presenters address their audiences at a logical level by throwing lots of complex information at them. The results are often contrary to what is desired. The same information told through story is immensely more effective. Indeed, there is no dispute in the scholarly or practitioner communities regarding the persuasive power of storytelling. Consider this experiment conducted by Martin and Powers:

Martin and Powers (1979), testing the effectiveness of an advertisement for a winery, randomly assigned subjects to three groups. One group was shown statistical tables concerning the winemaking process, one was shown statistical tables and told a story, and the third was told the story only. The group shown only the statistical tables subsequently showed less commitment to the advertised brand while that group told only the story showed the most commitment. (McConkie & Boss, 1994)

The human brain is simply not inspired by logic alone. Research and practical experience shows that emotion has more to do with decision-making than previously thought (Damasio, 2001), yet only a handful of the most successful business presenters intuitively understand and exploit this phenomenon. The irony is this: while most presenters tend to provide logic-based rhetoric, listeners are inherently persuaded to action by emotion-based stories, giving rise to a *perception gap* like the one in Figure 6.5. While many presenters speak through logic, most listeners hear through their emotions.

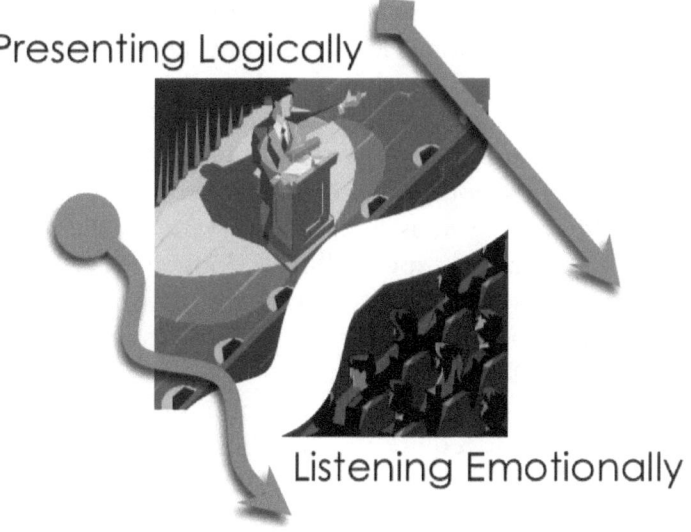

Figure 6.5. Perception gap b/w logical presenters & emotional listeners

Many business presenters erroneously believe that the more product features and benefits they showcase, the more receptive the client will be. As we discussed earlier, there is an inherent problem in assuming that product features and benefits alone will map to a client's needs without involving them in a bi-directional, emotion-based dialog. For most bullet-point presenters, features and benefits are the starting point and core headlines of their business presentations. A standard feature/benefit presentation starts with an introduction of the vendor's company, the business landscape or competitive environment, and then a listing of each feature and benefit of their product as topic headings. This approach is dangerously 'product-centric', meaning that it is not as 'customer-centric' as it could be, and clients won't see or feel a clear connection with their own business needs. Regardless of the details provided, the audience is usually left asking, "So what?" Time and extra care must be taken to ensure that clients can tell their stories so you can help them to clarify their needs. There can only be a meaningful discussion of *value* and benefits when there is agreement on both sides of the boardroom about the exact nature of a client's needs.

It is hardly surprising that most sales, marketing, and service professionals tend to focus on presenting information in lieu of persuading audiences at an emotional level. For one thing, ever since Descartes boldly proclaimed, "I think, therefore I am," western culture has overwhelmingly maintained a logic-first approach when dealing with human decision-making. Secondly, very few people ever learn persuasive business presentation skills in school, and when they join the work force, much of the training they receive is focused on turning them into product specialists, not persuasion experts. Finally, look at what people have to sell in today's information age. In a global economy that is increasingly more service-oriented, most people have to essentially "sell the invisible" (Beckwith, 1997).

In today's ever-changing, over-informed, global business landscape, most products and services that require repeated business presentations are not only intangible, they are also complex in nature. Whether you sell high technology products, financial services, computer hardware, software, or real estate and mortgages, you must learn how to make complex information appear simple, tangible and persuasive. You must turn the business presentation process into a unique competitive advantage and differentiate yourself from your competitors. It is only through the conduit of trust that effective persuasion is possible. Science shows that the human species is biologically hard-wired to seek trust first, before dealing with features and benefits (Goleman, Boyatzis, & McKee, 2002). People want confidence that your proposed solutions will truly solve their problems. People don't want features and benefits. They want trust.

YOU ARE WHAT YOU BELIEVE

We've just gone over the three most common myths that keep people from developing the skills required to master the art and science of influence through business presentations. Now let's take a look at you. Up until now, what have been your thoughts and beliefs regarding business presentations? Have you ever stopped to ask yourself that question? Do you believe, for example, that you have to be an eloquent public speaker before you can influence people in presentations? Do you practice listening as much as speaking? Do you consciously or unconsciously believe that preparation isn't that important? Do you believe that you can 'wing it' and over time, things will magically fall into place? Or do you believe that your audiences are only interested in 'serious' business logic, data, and information, and that storytelling would fall into the category of 'fluffy' stuff – which would have no impact in your mission-critical business meetings?

If you want to start winning more clients through business presentations, your first step is to examine these beliefs, and *change* them! Faulty beliefs can only hold you back, and cannot support any positive change. You must get rid of self-limiting thoughts and focus your energies on one clear goal – connecting and engaging emotionally with your audience. You must also believe in the power of storytelling to help you do that, and you must become a practitioner of communicating through questions that encourage your audience to share their stories with you. Above all, you must believe this: your ability to share and listen to stories, connect emotionally, and inspire listeners through this process is not just a 'nice to have' skill. Mastering the art and science of influence through business presentations is a sine qua non. It is a 'must-have' skill set that can positively impact your life, your career, and your hopes for success in the world of business.

CASE STUDY

THE PARABLE OF THE EMOTIONAL SHOE

A fellow PhD learner once invited me to coach some Minnesota-based Somali teenagers on how to create and deliver a business presentation. The purpose of their presentation was for submission to an Urban League and Microsoft-sponsored entrepreneurship competition. The winner of that competition would get $15,000 and a chance to have their start-up idea funded by Microsoft. When I arrived at their meeting place, I found the teenagers feverishly practicing their lines from a thirty-page PowerPoint® presentation that was jam-packed with technical information. After I watched them for a while, my fellow learner asked me, "What would you do to improve this presentation?" and I said, "Throw it away."

Everyone was shocked. They had spent at least a month trying to come up with those slides, and each person had their lines and routines down tight. Clearly, they were not expecting me to suggest getting rid of their hard work. I explained to them that people don't *hear* information; they *feel* it. To demonstrate my point, I asked their best speaker to try to sell me his shoe. He took it off, and held it high above the table for all to see. And then heroically, he began to list off all of its wonderful attributes, such as the fact that it was a Nike, it was still brand new and shiny, and the fact that it had several other great features that no other brand possessed. When he was done, I asked everyone to tell me if they would buy his shoe based on that presentation. No one would buy his shoe.

So I took his shoe and stood at the head of the table to further demonstrate my point to them. In a loud, pain-filled voice I announced: "Every minute while we sit in our comfortable chairs here in America, a child back home in Africa dies of hunger!" holding the shoe ever higher, I continued, still in a loud voice, "This shoe! Simple as it may seem, was a dream come true for me when I stepped foot on this soil, this America, this land of freedom! Just like you, I was once one of those children, deep in a Somali village. Buy this shoe for only $10 dollars, and place it as a reminder in your home and in your heart that the future will be brighter than the past. Together, it will serve as a symbol to remind us that we must continue to work hard to make this world..." Here I paused for dramatic effect, and then continued: "A better place!"

One of the students had a tear in her eye. I asked if anyone would buy the shoe and sure enough, they all said YES!

What did I do differently? I completely ignored the "information" about the shoe, and knowing my audience, I focused on attaching an emotional benefit to the shoe. I was no longer selling a shoe; I was selling an emotion! After our training sessions, those teens went on to compete in the Microsoft competition, and after winning at all the local levels, traveled to New York, where they won the National competition, a chance to be funded by Microsoft, and $15,000 in cash - more money than they had ever seen in their entire lives!

This may be a bit of an extreme example, but the moral of the story is this; although humankind has long since left the jungle, our minds, still powerfully emotional, have not. We still make decisions governed by the same emotional laws that our ancestors were subject to in the jungle. Current, scientific brain research does not lie: we still *jungle-talk*, and in business and sales presentations, this phenomenon is seen clearly and powerfully. If you're like most business people, you've invested heavily to make sure your prospects or clients understand the value of what you're selling. Yet when it's time to communicate that value, most business presentations are still high on information and low on emotion - which is the critical component that leads to a buying decision. Don't leave your clients' buying decisions to PowerPoint® and information overload. Help make it easy for your clients to buy what you sell. Help them *feel* like buying.

CHAPTER 6 SUMMARY

IT'S ABOUT CONNECTING, NOT PUBLIC SPEAKING

- Current neuroscience has confirmed it: contrary to what most people think, we are feeling beings that think, not thinking beings that feel.

- There are three core truths about business presentations, which you must internalize in order to achieve persuasion.

1. An influential business presentation is not about dynamic public speaking; it's about connecting through natural storytelling and storylistening.

2. Loading up a graphically pleasing bullet-point presentation will not make you more persuasive. You cannot 'wing-it', or 'fake-it-till-you-make-it' – you must understand how influence works, adjust your mindset, and become consciously competent at connecting with clients.

3. People overwhelmingly present from a paradigm of logic, and ignore the emotional realm through which audiences listen. It's not about features and benefits. It's about emotional connection.

•   Einstein was right. Logic is but the servant; when it comes to decision-making, emotions are the master.

EXERCISES

•   What are your beliefs regarding the business presentation medium? Do you rely on PowerPoint® to convey your points?

•   Write down the emotions you experience before, during, and after business presentations.

•   How much preparation do you put into your presentation delivery? (Not your PowerPoint® slides) Do you rehearse? If so, how? In front of a mirror, a mock audience? Write down how you prepare for a business presentation.

•   Next time you intend to convince or persuade in a conversation, resist telling facts alone. Instead, try telling a story that conveys emotions while making your point, and see what happens!

7. The Biology Of Influence

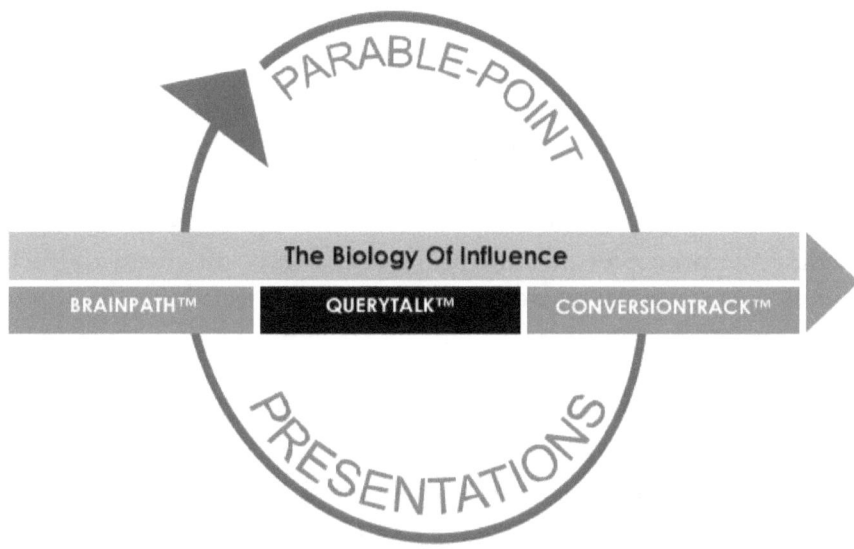

"People exercise an unconscious selection in being influenced."
- T. S. ELLIOT

Have you ever noticed those select few individuals who seem to have a knack for getting people to do what they want? Have you ever worked with someone who is excellent at sales, interpersonal skills, or is irresistibly eloquent and influential? Are you one of those people? If you are, you're among a very select few, because most people are not naturally that way. What about the rest of us? Thankfully, as far as nature versus nurture debates go, some people may be 'born influencers', but the rest of us can also learn how to become more influential by simply studying and adopting the clues left behind by these lucky few. Scientists have found that there are biological underpinnings to the concept of influence, and it has been documented now in countless experiments. This chapter will review the art of persuasion and influence, with the underlying scientific research as a backdrop.

As part of this discussion, we will cover the following topics:

- A formula for Influence
- The Neuron Brain
- Social Resonance
- The Six Principles of Influence

At the end of this discussion, you will be able to start consciously including the principles of influence into the way you create and deliver business presentations, regardless of whether you are a born influencer or not.

A FORMULA FOR INFLUENCE

I once heard the story of a man who visited his friend and discovered that his friend's dog was moaning and groaning constantly in the doorway.

Said he to his friend: "Why is your dog moaning and groaning?"

Said his friend: "Because it is sitting on a nail."

"Then why doesn't he just get up and walk away?"

His friend pondered the question for a moment and then, as if rediscovering the light bulb, he exclaimed, "The nail is hurting only badly enough to cause the dog to moan and groan, but not bad enough for the dog to get up and walk away!" (Brown, 2004)

Les Brown's 'parable of the moaning dog' showcases how people spend most of their lives naturally avoiding pain and looking for pleasure. If the outcomes in their lives produce pain, such as sadness, poverty, etc., then they will associate the memory of pain to those activities. Similarly, if things cause pleasure, such as eating, smiling etc., they will associate pleasure to those things. If things don't hurt badly enough, people don't have enough reason to make changes.

B.F. Skinner constructed a theory of *operant conditioning*, which essentially states that one's behavior can be modified by the use of consequences. For example, if the dog in our parable were able to receive greater punishment that reached a certain threshold of pain because of sitting on that nail, it would get up and move. However, without that punishment, (in fact, with the ongoing positive reinforcement of sitting on the nail and feeling no pain), the dog will continue to sit there. This is because the dog doesn't yet make the association of extreme pain to a nail that simply doesn't hurt. If you want to get the dog to move, you have to first make it feel the pain. The same goes for people. If you want to make a person change their behavior, you have to magnify their emotions regarding the potential consequences of their actions.

This phenomenon is critical to business presentations. If you are able to help your audience feel enough pain by reinforcing certain consequences about a pending decision, they will avoid making that decision. At the same time, if you are able to make them feel and understand all the positive rewards that can result from another decision, that reinforcement will lead them to a different set of decisions. This concept of operant conditioning is the basis for my *formula of influence.* The methodology that you use for magnifying these various emotions is found in carefully constructed questions and parables. Here is my formula for influence:

The formula for **influence** states that your ability to influence a prospect's decision depends on the intensity of **emotion** they feel regarding their needs, and the feasibility of the **action** plan that you have provided them.

$$I = E + A$$

Influence = Emotion + Action

I = influence
E = emotion
A = action

This formula basically means that if you ever want to persuade people in a business presentation, do some prior research on their pains and needs, and then maximize those emotions through the use of stories. At the same time, you have to make sure that your stories allude to a specific plan of action. If you are able to structure a series of stories that reinforce their emotions, while supplying the first action steps they can take, you will find your audiences being much more inspired to take action. As the popular saying goes, *good* selling is not sales at all: it is the process of simply '*helping*' your customer to buy.

How then can you implement this law of influence? As we've just discussed, the best way to persuade people in a business meeting is to highlight and elevate their emotions regarding either the pain or pleasure associated with a specific course of action, while also showing them a clear action plan for achieving their goals. However, simply telling people how they should feel or what they should do is not effective because they do not inherently start out by trusting what you are saying. The best way to increase people's emotions regarding either pain or pleasure it is to have them increase it *themselves*!

If you encourage people, through careful questions, to tell you how badly they will feel if they take a certain action, they will feel it much more powerfully than if you tell them. Similarly, if you allow them to tell you how good they would feel if they took another course of action, they will feel it more realistically as well. Customers are predisposed to more strongly believe whatever they tell you, much more than anything you can ever tell them. Because they are participating in the discussion, they will have a sense of ownership of the final outcomes, and their conclusions will stick much more powerfully in their minds.

In every business presentation, ask **questions** to encourage your clients to tell you stories. Then, ask more questions to dig deeper, and raise the emotions of pain or pleasure associated with a certain decision. Make sure to also provide specific **action** steps that will lead to success for your clients. This process of 'talking through questions' is what I call 'QueryTalk', and we will cover it in greater detail in chapter 8 – The parable point presentation system.

THE NEURON BRAIN

German-born architect Ludwig Mies van de Rohe is sometimes credited with the popular phrase, "God is in the details," which points to the fact that the truth of any matter is usually found in close, detailed analysis. Greek philosopher Plato once suggested broadly that humans are essentially a mind-body dichotomy in which the mind is elevated to the status of an immortal entity. However, today's cutting-edge neuroscientists are now 'looking at the details', and are challenging the notion of a spirit-mind that cannot be explained through the mechanics of bio-chemical interactions. One such scientist, Nobel Laurate Frances Crick, claims the following:

> You, your joys and your sorrows, your memories and your ambitions, your sense of personal identity and free will, are in fact no more than the behavior of a vast assembly of nerve cells and their associated molecules" (Crick, 1994).

Another renowned professor, neuroscientist Michael Gazzaniga, puts it even more succinctly by saying: "You are your brain."

Indeed, state-of-the-art neuro-imaging technologies are now showing this way of seeing the world to be true. We are now able to put people through a scanner and watch the neural connections of certain areas of the brain become 'excited' in response to certain stimuli. Experiments have shown that our brains are a mass of neurons firing off electrochemical impulses as they receive information from the world around us. Since the brain can be explained biologically, can we then also demonstrate that stories are a catalyst for decision-making? According to neuroscience, the answer is yes. Scientists can now show that we are hardwired to respond more to stories than to *flat* data and information. According to Dr. Guy Claxton, some neuroscientists believe the brain has certain "learning amplifiers," which are laser-focused and waiting for stories:

> There are many cells in the human brain – the 'mirror neurons' – that automatically get ready to initiate an action that they have just seen someone else do: so many, that it begins to look as if we are hard-wired to pick up the habits of those around us. As the brain builds up a stock of mental models of different people, so we become able to 'put ourselves in their shoes', and explore different scenarios. (Claxton, 2004, Para 8)

This new perspective explains why we now have emerging fields such as neuromarketing, in which people study how the brain reacts when potential clients are presented with different kinds of advertising. This new branch of marketing concerns itself with helping organizations identify the most powerful, emotion-laden communication and go-to-market ideas. Stories seem to inspire emotion inside these neurons, helping your listeners see things from your perspective, which is the first and most crucial step toward influence.

> Our minds are made of millions of neurons – little electro-chemical nodes that become active and excited, connecting and reconnecting whenever we listen to stories that make us think, learn, or experience emotion.
>
> Parables are the best way to **activate** those emotional neurons during a business presentation.

If neuromarketers can take advantage of brain-based methodologies to better target their marketing campaigns, why can't business presenters? The fact is this: if you could watch the way a listener's neurons react during your business presentation, you would probably discover that they respond more powerfully to stories than to factual information. Storytelling is the means by which a business presenter can encourage listeners to *identify* with a particular point that needs to be made. Hearing and seeing facts alone is one-dimensional. Identifying with something becomes personal, and creates a stronger, more emotional connection.

SOCIAL RESONANCE

I had just settled back into my seat on a Boeing 747 as it flew effortlessly over Europe, en route to Minneapolis. I was returning from a week-long series of business presentations, and was physically and emotionally drained. As the waiter came over to inquire if I would like a drink, we heard the captain's voice calmly announce that we were going to be turning around and heading back to Amsterdam. He pointed out that we should not be alarmed by the two streams of fuel that were gushing out of the engines on both wings, and that we were at that point, effectively flying on three engines instead of four! I began to tremble! Did I hear him just say that one engine had failed? Yes. That is essentially what he had said, albeit in a calm voice. Frantically, I looked at the man seated next to me, but he was still sleeping, and I could see that the person on the other aisle had heard the announcement as well, and was extremely disturbed. Finally, I turned to the flight attendant, to see exactly what she might be feeling, and that was when my worst fears were confirmed. Her eyebrows were raised, and her mouth remained slightly open in shock. She was clearly emotionally disturbed! She quickly scurried away, back from whence she came. In that split moment, I inherited her emotion, and became terribly afraid. Prior to that, I wasn't quite sure what to feel. I had been searching for social resonance - an emotion to depend on.

There is a popular physics experiment that showcases a similar phenomenon called sympathetic resonance. If you place two piano tuning forks of identical pitch next to each other and strike one of them, the second fork will begin to vibrate as well. This phenomenon occurs because sound waves are carried as particle vibrations through the air and will register at the same exact frequency on a remote identical instrument. While this may seem like a physical, mechanical phenomenon, in fact, the emerging field of social neuroscience is showing that this same kind of thing happens to human beings. Daniel Goleman's new book, *Social Intelligence* makes a surprising new claim about "neural wi-fi" – pointing once again to the power of the mind's 'mirror neurons':

> Mirror neurons make emotions contagious, letting the feelings we witness flow through us, helping us get in synch and follow what's going on. We "feel" the other in the broadest sense of the word: sensing their sentiments, their movements, their sensations, and their emotions as they act inside us. (Goleman, 2006, p. 42)

This phenomenon can be seen in business presentations everywhere. Most people don't realize just how much power they have to control the feelings, emotions, and energy of audience members. As you present, audience members are all searching for a neural frequency to tune into. If you show positive emotions, they will follow you; if you show negative emotions, they will also feel negative feelings. A classic experiment conducted by Yale professor Sigal Barsade revealed an interesting finding which he described as "emotional contagion" (Barsade, 2002). Two groups of managers were placed in two different rooms to make critical bonus decisions. In each room, unbeknownst to the groups, a seasoned actor was placed who contributed to the meetings. One was confrontational and negative, while the other was upbeat and positive. At the end of the experiment, the room with the confrontational actor ended up with people feeling confrontational, while the other ended up with people feeling positive. The decisions that were made in each group were in line with how they felt.

> Social resonance states that emotions are **contagious** at a biological level.
>
> You are in more control over your listeners' emotions than you think. If you want them to smile – then you yourself must smile!

This idea is not entirely new, as it echoes some of the 'above and below the line' theories of contagious energy that were proposed by Dr. David Hawkins in his book, *Power vs. Force*. Dr. Hawkins found that there are several levels of energy and consciousness that can be transmitted between people in a group setting. He mapped these levels on a scale of consciousness and divided them into two groups above a middle line representing 'courage', which he called a "critical response point"(Hawkins, 1995, p. 70). In his scale, courage registered at 200. Above the energy field of courage were feelings such as willingness, reason, love, joy, peace and so on. Below the courage line were emotions such as anger, fear, grief, apathy, guilt, shame, etc. Figure 7.1 shows this distribution of energy levels.

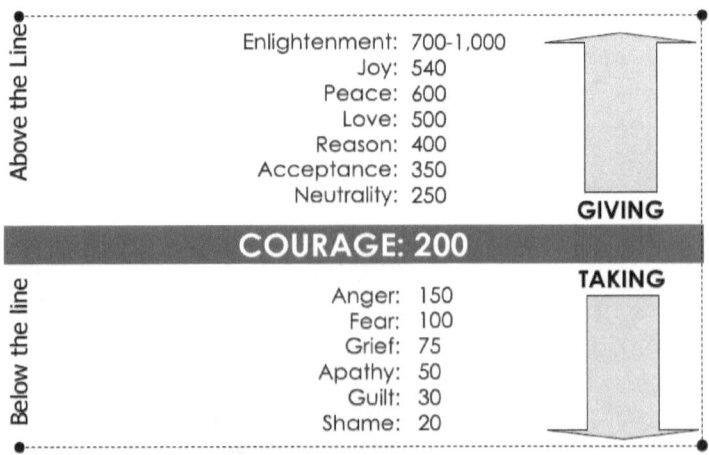

Figure 7.1. Adaptation of Hawkins's Map of Consciousness

Essentially, when you project feelings that are 'below the line' your audience will feel that way as well. If you remain 'above the line' in the way you talk, move, and act, so will your audience. Social resonance dictates that people's brains are involuntarily 'watching' your every move, listening to your words, and looking for ways to 'connect' to what you are feeling and saying. If you use this baseline knowledge to manage the feelings in your audience, you will get much better results, decisions, and outcomes than if you never knew you had this law on your side.

THE SIX PRINCIPLES OF PERSUASION

In his book, *Influence*, professor Robert Cialdini painstakingly laid out the scientific case for a general theory of influence. By looking at the work of behavioral scientists over the past five decades, he concluded that there are at least at least six identifiable principles behind the art of persuasion, and that anyone can learn them if they wanted to. In a Harvard Business Review article, Cialdini (2001) stated:

> For the past five decades, behavioral scientist have conducted experiments that shed considerable light on the way certain interactions lead people to concede, comply, or change. This research shows that persuasion works by appealing to a limited set of deeply rooted human drives and needs, and it does so in predictable ways. Persuasion, in other words, is governed by basic principles that can be taught, learned, and applied. By mastering these principles, executives can bring scientific rigor to the business of securing consensus, cutting deals, and winning concessions. (p. 74)

According to Cialdini, The six principles of Influence he identified from the research literature are:

1. The Principle of Liking
2. The Principle of Reciprocity
3. The Principle of Social Proof
4. The Principle of Consistency
5. The Principle of Authority

6. The Principle of Scarcity

The Principle of Liking basically states that "people like those who like them" (p. 74). In a business presentation, you should therefore seize every opportunity to increase your 'likeability'. Research shows that there are two main ways of doing this; (a) highlight similarities, and (b) praise your client. The more you showcase where you are similar with your audience, and the more you provide them positive feedback, the more they will like you, and therefore, be open to influence from you.

The Principle of Reciprocity means: "people repay in kind" (p.75). As we've discussed earlier, giving is so much more powerful than getting. Several experiments have shown that people will feel strongly obligated to give you something if you have given them something first. Essentially, the moral behind this principle is that you must give what you want to receive. As we discussed earlier, one of the best things you can give your audience is a chance to get involved and share their stories.

The Principle of Social Proof is a powerful indicator of how peer power works. Studies have shown that people will "follow the lead of similar others" (p. 75). In the publishing industry, you will frequently find a book with the headline: "From the World Renowned Author of the New York Times Bestselling Book." The reason for this is because the publishers know that readers are more inspired to buy something that others have bought, than a brand new book that hasn't been proven. The moral of this principal in business presentations is this: instead of just telling clients about your features and benefits, tell them a story about how someone else has achieved an impressive return on investment by implementing your solution.

The Principle of Consistency states that "people will align with their clear commitments" (p. 76). Essentially, if you can get people to commit to something, especially in a public, active, and involuntary manner, they are more likely to follow through. One of the ways this can work in a business presentation is to get your audience talking to you right from the beginning. Ask each person to introduce himself or herself, agree to participate, and state what he or she wishes to learn from the meeting. Not only does this help you target their needs better, it helps put them on track to actually work hard to participate and learn.

The Principle of Authority means that "people defer to experts" (p. 77). It doesn't hurt if you let your audience know how many years you have spent in a specific field so that they can rely on your expertise and credibility. In a business presentation, obviously you should not be arrogant, but don't be too laid back either. Don't assume that your expertise is patently obvious. You have to make it known right up front.

The Principle of Scarcity states that "people want more of what they can have less of" (p. 78). The nature of the human animal seems to be that we value things more if they either seem to be more expensive or less available. I have been in sales situations where it was more effective to show a client why something may not be right for her than it was to try to sell her on it! In business presentations, it is important to highlight your unique benefits and exclusive information.

A QUICK NOTE ABOUT ETHICS

It is important to know that although there is immense power in the ability to influence people, it should never be used unethically. No one appreciates being manipulated. Not only can it hurt your reputation immensely, it is simply not right, and it is bad business to boot. There is a fine line however, between manipulation, and genuinely using the principles of influence in your favor. Clients are looking for you to help make their process of buying easier, and the nature and biology of the human animal simply dictates that you have to use certain principles to get them outside of their barricades and more open to your offering. So be cautious when using the power of influence. Dishonest tactics only work in the short term. It is in your best interest to always be ethical, for the long-term survival and success of yourself, your clients, and your entire organization.

CASE STUDY

A PARABLE OF 'HOW'

Carl Sewell is the owner of one of the most successful car dealerships in the United States. To make a point about how his company works, and his undying dedication to customer service, he tells the following parable;

> "We have an excellent customer who lives half the year in Dallas and the other half in France. When she was coming back from Paris last year she called us up and said that she planned to spend some time in New York before returning home, but she didn't want to rent a car there. She said all New York rental cars were dirty and smelled of cigarette smoke. She wanted to know if we could rent a car for her in Dallas and have someone drive it to new York, and turn it over to her there. ... We could and we did."

(Sewell & Brown, 1990, p. 11)

CHAPTER 7 SUMMARY

THE BIOLOGY OF INFLUENCE

- There is a universal formula for influence: $I = E + A$. (Influence – Emotion + Action)
- This means that Influence is the result of helping your audience feel how much they need something, (emotion), and then providing them with the specific actions they need to take in order to achieve their ends.

- "You are your brain." Neuro-imaging systems show that people have 'mirror neurons' that are hardwired to respond to stories.

- Social resonance means that emotions are contagious. You can manage your audience's emotions by the way you project your own. If you project confidence and hope, your audience will feel the same. However, if you are nervous, they will be nervous along with you.

- Cialdini's six principles of influence – liking, reciprocity, social proof, consistency, authority, and scarcity – are all available to you. You will increase your ability to influence clients if you design these emotion-touching principles into presentations.

EXERCISE

Next time you are in a presentation, try the formula for Influence.

Influence = Emotion + Action

Ask questions that will liberate your client's emotions about the advantages and disadvantages of a certain decision. Keep asking questions and digging deeper until the client convinces themselves of the right course of action – your solution! Also, make sure to provide them a specific course of action – some small steps they can take right now toward your solution.

8. The Science Of Inspirational Storytelling

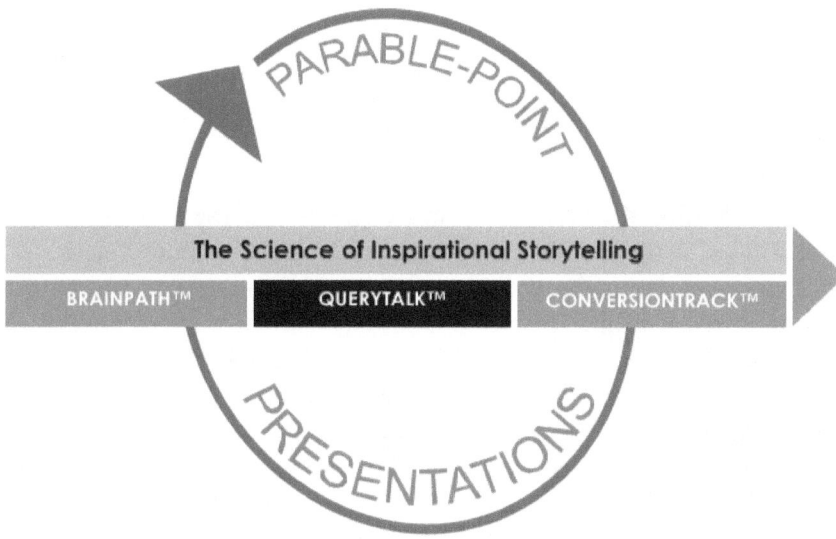

"The fly that has no counselor will follow the corpse to the grave."
- IGBO PROVERB

One of my earliest memories is from when I was six years old in Minneapolis. I had just moved to America and was newly introduced to the children in my Como Avenue neighborhood. One day, there was a soccer game going on at the park, and I was invited to play. I vividly remember the way all the kids cheered and shouted my name, and I was anxious to demonstrate my skills. After all, I shared a name with Pelè, the greatest soccer player of all time, and I was eager to live up to the reputation that preceded me. Someone passed the ball to me and I dribbled the first person, and the next, and somehow, I even managed to get past a third person! Now I had the goalpost in my sights and no one was near me. The crowd roared! This was my chance to prove to these kids that I was worth every inch of the name Pelè! I took careful aim before anyone could get close to me and – I scored my first goal ever! Excitedly, I ran to the sidelines with my hands up in the air, and that's when I noticed something strange. The kids weren't cheering any more. Instead, they were laughing and rolling on the ground. You see, I had scored a goal alright, but I had scored in the wrong goalpost! I had just demonstrated an important truth. Despite my passion and speed, I knew nothing about the rules of the game, and couldn't play soccer to save my life! Through that shame, I learned a simple guiding principle I have followed since then: knowing how to run and kick a ball doesn't mean you are good at soccer. If you want to *win* a game, you have to understand its rules.

Understanding the science behind something is the process of getting to know how it works so that you can be more effective at it. While science has long been the way we explore and understand the world we live in, its most useful application is arguably in providing us with rules, laws, or building blocks upon which we can quickly create meaningful tools to achieve our human purposes. For example, as a result of Newton's laws, we have built cars and airplanes. As a result of Faraday's laws, we now have electricity, and by extension, computers and the Internet. As a result of Einstein's laws, we are beginning to understand the universe in new, paradigm-breaking ways. Similarly, if you understand the laws governing why the art of storytelling is one of the best agents of human inspiration and persuasion, you will be able to build your presentation skills to a point of competence. This chapter is devoted to discussing the science, laws, and organizing principles for how storytelling plays a central role in getting people inspired to action. Here are the laws, which together form what I call the *science of inspirational storytelling*:

1. The law of Storytelling
2. The law of Storylistening
3. The law of the Emotional Brain
4. The law of Viral Storytelling

Let us now go through a process of describing each law. By understanding how stories and parables work to make your points in business presentations, you will be well on your way to implementing the rules behind the game of persuasive business presentations. You'll be competent and purposeful, and you will never have to do what I did in my first soccer game: score in the *wrong* goal post!

THE LAW OF STORYTELLING

A long time ago, long before automobiles, electricity and reality television, Darwin's bushman sat on a large pile of rocks in the cool of the night's air. He pulled a large handful of snuff from his goatskin bag, and without regard to the eager eyes watching him from below, he placed a pinch of it on a battle-worn thumb and thrust it deep into his left nostril. He followed with a humongous sneeze and a grunt of satisfaction as he wiped his fingers on his loincloth. Finally, he looked around him. The sky was dark and cloudless. Pitch black. He saw the stars above him; thousands upon thousands of them, as numerous as his wives and children who sat around him, anxiously waiting for the great man to speak. He wiped his nostrils again with his fingers, and took one last ceremonial pinch of snuff as his father had done before him; and his father's father had done before him; and so on and so on for millennia upon millennia of bushmen since the dawn of time. Finally, he began to tell the story of creation; the parable of how the bushmen of his tribe had conquered the wild and preserved all their lessons from fire-making to hunting and dancing; and how all these truths brought order to the lives they live today. Darwin's bushman was a natural storyteller. However, he was not just telling moonlight stories for fun. He was teaching, inspiring, and preserving his species.

Ever since Charles Darwin wrote the last of his four great books, *The Expression of Emotions in Man and Animals*, there has been a flurry of scientific activity to uncover the biological underpinnings of emotion, which he pursued as one of the greatest forms of evidence regarding the "unity of mankind" (Darwin, 1872). He offered the notion that all humans come from a similar source, not only because of biological and anthropological evidence, but because they share the same universal expressions for the biological function of emotion (Ekman, 1992). Through this evidence of 'basic emotions', Darwin was basically implying the following: when it comes to emotions, we are no different from early man. We are, and have always been – storytellers.

How then did our ancestors survive and thrive in their wild environments? How did they preserve their cultures, pass on best their practices, and eventually conquer nature itself? The answer is that these Bushmen told emotion-carrying stories. Throughout the ages, humankind has relied on emotion for decision-making, and has used the power of emotion-driven story and rhetoric as a central tool for survival. Several millennia of conditioning have helped to evolve our species into a story-loving, emotional society. Indeed, the greatest influencers of all time were storytellers. Jesus told stories. Mohammed told stories. Buddha told stories. Details may fade over time, but the collective memories of ancient civilizations that have survived are those preserved through stories. Eons of storytellers can't be wrong. Storytelling is the key to influence!

> The law of storytelling states that the human animal is persuaded to action mostly at an emotional level.
>
> Parables are short stories that make points – the best agents for **conveying** action-causing emotions.

The reason stories are so powerful as a persuasive communication tool can be boiled down to the following facts:

- Stories make points memorable.
- Stories persuade indirectly: they don't push, they pull.
- Stories offer proof: they don't just tell, they show.
- Stories inspire empathy, and can replace a disbelieving mindset.
- Stories create 'Aha!'s through metaphor.
- Stories are viral: people love to repeat great stories.
- Stories connect with the emotions, and make logic easier to accept.

Through the use of metaphor, stories transport us to a seemingly trance-like state of 'experiencing' what we are hearing. The mind works by cross-checking, validating, disputing, or associating prior experiences it has in memory with what is being spoken at any given moment.

Essentially, people understand things better in metaphor because the images provided through story help them to see a clearer picture of the point you are making. Stories therefore move us to action in ways that facts have never been able to.

> "In a two hour speech, people will [only] remember a two-minute story"
>   – Goodman (2004)

Not only is storytelling important in business presentations, it is crucial to tell the right story at the right time. Part 3 will showcase three of the most important stories you must have in your arsenal: the parables of 'who', 'why', and 'how'. Try this next time you are speaking to a group of people: instead of sharing facts, lead with a story that indirectly makes your point, and you will see that their learning process will be more connected, and *meaningful*. Throughout history, stories have been the most natural and effective tool for sharing experiences, persuading listeners, and protecting the species; yet in today's world, they have been unfortunately squeezed out of business presentations by data and bullet-points. The parable point approach to business presentations is simple: use stories, parables and metaphor, not bullets, for making points that inspire action. If you want to persuade people to action, never start a meeting with facts. Always start with a story.

THE LAW OF STORYLISTENING

I once went to a business presentation given by Dr. Manny Steil, who is an expert on the subject of listening. He called the session, "You've Got Questions? So Do I!" Prior to the meeting, he sent an email to all the attendants, encouraging them to prepare at least one question to share with him and the rest of the audience. Here is the content of that email:

I look forward to spending a productive Fireside Forum on Friday with each of you. "You Got Questions? So Do I!" is designed to advance the professional insights and practices of every participant.

To maximize our morning, I invite each of you to come prepared with a single 'Powerful Question' you would like to explore. If needed, I have prepared 25 pointed questions for each of you, so there will be no wasted time. Together we should have many answers. (Steil, 2006)

The meeting itself was very unique, and it was one of the most productive meetings I have ever attended. Throughout the meeting, instead of telling us things, Dr. Steil asked us questions! Everyone had a chance to speak and contribute. At the end of the meeting, I could see from looking around the room that everyone felt that the meeting had met all their requirements. What this demonstrated to me is this: people enjoy talking! They don't come to meetings just to listen. If given a chance, they will express themselves, tell you their stories and become much more fulfilled in the process.

"The person who knows only his side of an issue knows neither side." – Cicero (Roman politician and orator, 106-43 BCE)

The greatest business presentation is a listening session.

When I approached Dr. Steil at the end of the meeting to thank him for such a wonderful and useful session, he told me that his approach to talking through questions and listening is driven by a mantra that is best captured by Rudyard Kipling's quote:

"I keep six honest serving men; they taught me all I knew. There names are What and Why and When and How and Where and Who."
 - Rudyard Kipling

The field of psychology is certainly one that adopts the listening approach wholeheartedly. Also, in life coaching, you find people who understand the value of good listening. Encourage and allow your clients to tell you stories and ask questions during business meetings. (Many would like to leave questions till the end, but this shuts out the audience.) By giving them permission to tell you stories, you can help them to uncover a deeper diagnosis of their business challenges. The process of listening will help them drop their guard, and will increase the mutual empathy in the boardroom. At the end of the day, it is smart to ask questions and listen, lest one is branded as thinking she knows it all. As the popular saying goes, the client knows best. Perhaps this sentiment is best articulated by Carl Rogers, a famous psychologist who famously stated, "It is the client who knows what hurts, what directions to go, what problems are crucial, what experiences have been deeply buried."

THE LAW OF THE EMOTIONAL BRAIN

Once upon a time there was a stubborn fly that employed the service of a counselor to keep him out of trouble. One day, he found a corpse lying in a coffin, and couldn't resist the temptation to jump in and help himself to a meal. The counselor told him that after careful analysis, he had concluded that this was a bad idea, but instead they got into a heated argument. They started shouting at each other and exchanging curses until the fly announced in a loud voice, "You're fired!" Dejected, the counselor was forced to leave. Finally free of an adviser, the fly jumped into the coffin with the corpse and began to feast heartily. Several hours later, the fly realized that it had become rather dark in the coffin. He lifted his head and flew upward for more light. However, he was amazed to find that there was no more light, no more sky, no more anything. The coffin's lid had been closed, and he was now six feet under - eternally buried with the corpse.

This ancient Igbo parable makes the point that "a fly that has no counselor will follow the corpse to the grave." The modern interpretation is what science has now demonstrated to be true: we have two brains that work together. Even more amazingly, they can also function independently of each other when split apart. Essentially, the human brain works like 'split-brain', much like the analogy of the fly and the counselor. The fly represents the right brain, which is emotional and intuitive, while the counselor represents the left brain, which is more logical and analytical. Scientific experimentation has shown that these two brain hemispheres are responsible for different types of information processing, yet, in order to survive as a species, we need them to coexist.

In the 1970's, Michael Gazzaniga et al witnessed a groundbreaking discovery that has dictated the way we understand the workings of the 'split brain' ever since. They witnessed a man whose brain had been literally divided into two in order to provide him relief from epileptic seizures. When they conducted several experiments on him, they reached some startling conclusions: both brains were different and independent in terms of how they processed information. Gazzaniga (1998) describes their conclusions from split-brain research:

> Ultimately, we discovered that the two hemispheres control vastly different aspects of thought and action. Each half has its own specialization and thus its own limitations and advantages. The left brain is dominant for language and speech. The right excels at visual-motor tasks. The language of these findings has become part of our culture: writers refer to themselves as left-brained, visual artists as right-brained. (para 4)

Their conclusions essentially described what we now know as the logical left brain, versus the emotional right brain. The left brain was shown to be much more conscious than the right brain, implying that a good portion of the emotions we feel – in the right brain – are unconscious. At the same time, the logical decisions that are made by the left brain are somehow being strongly influenced by this 'sub-conscious' right brain. It is this interaction between the two brains that gives rise to how we arrive at our decisions.

The idea of a divided brain is certainly of interest, but the most relevant aspect of these scientific discoveries to the art of persuasion is the relative *power* of emotions. Emotions occur sub-consciously and are more influential in the process of making decisions than the logical mind. Regarding the powerful role of emotions in decision-making, acclaimed neuroscientist Joseph LeDoux stated in his book, *The Emotional Brain*:

> Emotions are things that happen to us rather than things we will to occur . . . once emotions occur they become powerful motivators of future behaviors. . . . They chart the course of moment-to-moment action, as well as set the sails toward long-term achievement" (LeDoux, 1998, p. 19).

Decision-making is therefore a combined process of thinking and feeling, almost like an oxymoronic process of *emotional logic* - both sides contributing to the final decision. Since powerful emotions can happen to us whether we know it or not, it sometimes it takes some considerable effort to tame them, as a rider might tame an animal. This analogy is echoed in the ancient Buddhist text, the *Dhamma-pada*, in which the Buddha is credited with describing the eternal struggle between the logical and emotional mind:

> This mind of mine went formerly wandering about as it liked, as it listed, as it pleased; but I shall now hold it in thoroughly, as the rider who holds the hook holds in the furious elephant. (326)

When you are in a business presentation, it is important to note that people are listening to you from their divided brains. One brain is listening emotionally, the other logically. To truly capture an audience's attention, you must speak to them in both modes, giving them more of a 'whole-brained' experience. While you may use facts and figures to speak to their logical mind, don't overdo it. Remember that the elephant, the fly, the subconscious emotional mind, is the more powerful 'brain'. You must also speak to people's emotions. If all you do is speak to the logical mind, the powerful elephant will not be moved to action, and your chances at persuasion will be highly diminished.

The law of emotional power states that there are two parts to the human brain involved whenever decisions are made: one is the conscious, logical mind, and the other is the more powerful, sub-conscious, emotional mind.

Parables are the best way to **simultaneously** inspire the emotional mind while making a point for the logical mind.

THE LAW OF VIRAL STORYTELLING

Once upon a time, a cross-functional software team was tasked with providing a final recommendation to their CEO about which software package the company should purchase in order to solve their growing information management problems. For years they had struggled with an in-house flat-record database application that was slow, cumbersome, and confusing, to say the least. One day, the team went to visit a remote branch of their company in a far away land, where they had no access to the internet, phones, or any means of communicating with headquarters. At this remote location, they saw the makings of what seemed a promising solution to their organizational software problem, but were unable to call anyone to get clarification on certain points so that they could arrive at a decision – and a decision had to be made at that critical point, or the opportunity would be lost!

So they decided to tell each other stories. They sat down in a circle and started telling each other the stories they could remember from all the meetings they had sat through with various vendors. Over and over again, the only stories they could remember came from a particular vendor. This vendor, (of course), used the parable point approach, and had used parables instead of bullet-points to describe his product's features and benefits – as opposed to the other companies that had just provided a bunch of sales facts. They finally arrived at a conclusion, fixed the problems, and returned triumphantly to headquarters. At the next meeting, the CEO asked which software package they ought to buy and the team members all looked at each other and smiled. Without hesitation, they recommended the vendor with the parable points over all the others. When it really mattered, his was the only product they could remember and describe.

Split brain research has yielded support to the question of memory retention. In six experiments exploring hemispheric memory differences in a patient who had undergone complete corpus callosum resection (meaning both brains were separated), neuroscientists were able to show that the right brain, (the emotional brain) was much better able to retain memories than the left (logical) brain (Metcalfe, Funnell, & Gazzaniga, 1995). This is not a surprising result for anyone who tells stories. It is common knowledge that people will easily forget facts, but will always remember stories. However, this reveals an important reason why business presenters ought to use stories and parables more often: facts don't stay in left-brain memory as well as stories stay in the right-brain, and what you remember has a lot to do with your decision-making process.

Beyond just being memorable, parables and stories have the innate capacity of encouraging their own *transfer*. In other words, they are viral. As we mentioned in chapter two, Dr. Richard Mayer, a professor of psychology at the University of California, conducted research that shows that this process of transfer produces *meaningful* learning - the highest form of learning possible (Mayer, 2002). Dr. Mayer explored three possible learning outcomes during presentations. The first outcome is what he called 'no learning'. The second he called 'rote' learning, and the third, which was the highest form of learning possible, he called 'meaningful' learning. When no learning occurs people are essentially unable to retain or remember anything that was presented to them. According to Dr. Mayer, an improvement on the no-learning outcome is rote learning. In this form of learning, people are able to remember what they were taught, but they are limited in the fact that they are unable to take that knowledge and transfer it to new situations. What this means is that what they have learned may indeed be memorable, but it has not become useful enough for them in their own lives to inspire them to reconstruct and reuse it in new situations. The best form of learning is when people are able to both retain and transfer the information that they have learned into new situations. People are encouraged and able to spread the stories they hear to others, like the gospel of Jesus, or like the cross-functional software team that solved their problems by remembering stories.

How then does one create meaningful learning? The way to do this is through a combination of telling stories, talking with questions, and encouraging audience participation. This approach helps you transfer your product information from short term (left-brain) memory, to long term (right-brain) memory.

In long sales cycles, it is difficult to get all the members of a decision-making team in one room at the same time. As a result, it is important that whatever you present to them remains planted solidly in their memory, and is short and interesting enough for those present to want to repeat it to others when you are not around. This word of mouth, viral process of spreading your ideas is at the heart of Malcolm Gladwell's book, *The Tipping Point*, in which he likened the spread of ideas to the spread of a virus among a human population. As he points out, "It is safe to say that word of mouth is – even in this age of mass communications and multimillion dollar advertising campaigns – still the most important form of human communication" (Gladwell, 2002, p. 32).

> The law of viral memory states that your audience members will remember and **repeat** what they learn best.
>
> Parables are the best way to 'employ' your audience to spread your message virally among their ranks via word of mouth.

This is certainly true of the viral spread of the gospel of Jesus. From an initial twelve disciples, we now have a religion whose followers easily make up 33% of the world's population. Jesus used parables as the method of transferring his information and recruiting listeners to follow him and spread the gospel. As we can see, that was certainly an effective marketing strategy! If you intend to persuade others, tell them modern parables, short stories that will connect to their emotional brains, stay locked in memory, and help them with decisions later on. Most important, these short stories will lend themselves to being easily repeated and passed on to other listeners within your target organization, who will in turn continue to spread your message of hope throughout their ranks. In a business presentation, instead of facts, figures, features and benefits, give your audience something they will remember. Give them parables and stories that will not only solve their problems, but will also spread like wildfire!

CASE STUDY

THE PARABLE OF "THE $125,000 THANK YOU"

Here's a viral parable that David Armstrong describes in his book *Managing By Storying Around*. This story helps to pass on one of the core values that his organization espouses to all its employees – by word of mouth.

"All companies go through tough times, and Armstrong, unfortunately, is no exception. In 1987, for the first time since the Depression, we put a wage freeze into effect to help us get through what looked like it would be a very difficult year.

Our employees were amazing. They accepted the freeze with very few complaints. "The company has always been fair with me" seemed to be the prevailing attitude. "Now it's my turn to be fair to the company."

A few months into the new year it looked like 1987 was going to be much better than projected. We decided that not only could we give everybody raises, but we could afford to make them retroactive. The back pay came to about $400 per employee.

We didn't give our employees that $400 by check. Instead, we called everybody into the recreation building where my father, company president, was standing behind a large table covered with a white sheet. He explained that since Armstrong was doing better than anticipated, the company wanted to share its good fortune.

With that, he lifted the sheet, and everyone saw that the table was covered with $10 bills – some 12,500 of them – stacked two feet high.

One by one, each employee came up, shook my dad's hand and those of the company's managers, and was told, "Thank you for your understanding." They walked away with forty crisp, new $10 bills.

If there's a point to be made, either good or bad, do it dramatically. People will remember."   (Armstrong, 1992, p. 55)

CHAPTER 8 SUMMARY

THE SCIENCE OF INSPIRATIONAL STORYTELLING

- The law of storytelling states that the human animal is persuade to action mostly at an emotional level, and parables and short stories are the best agents for conveying these action-causing emotions.

- Listening to clients' stories is just as important as telling your own. The combination of telling and listening to stories is the kind of interaction that makes for influence.

- The law of the emotional brain states that you need to address emotions at least as much as logic, facts and data in your presentations.

- The law of viral storytelling states that your audience will help you spread good business stories that make important points.

EXERCISE

- Have you heard a good corporate parable recently? What point did it make? Who told it? Were you influenced by it? Did it touch you emotionally? Write it down, and with the original teller's permission, tell it to others, and see if it has the same effect on them.

9. How To Create Your Own Business Parables

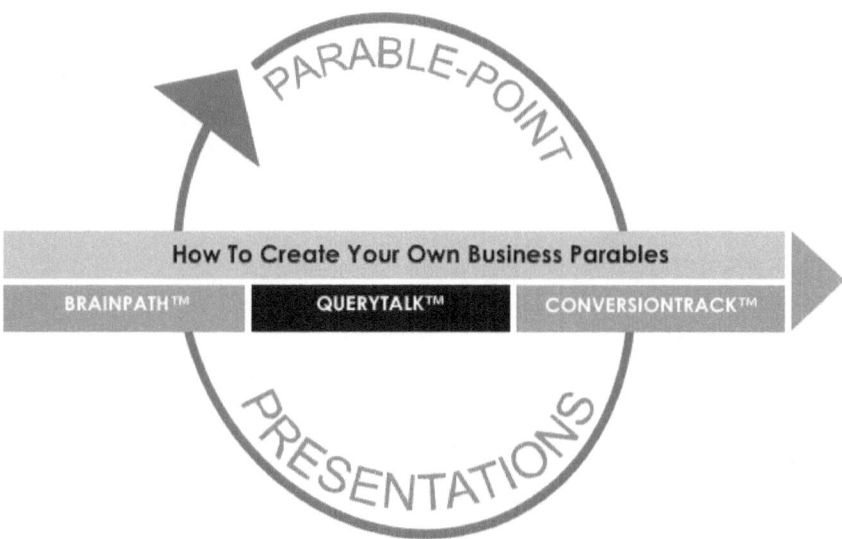

"It is said that a man's character is hidden beneath his tongue, because the tongue says what is in the heart."

- FRIEDLANDER, 1992, p. 31

So far, we have discussed the mindset needed for orienting yourself away from 'ME-centric' bullet-points, and moving you toward more influential and persuasive business storytelling. We've reviewed the science behind business narrative and parables so that you get a sense of how they work behind the scenes to influence the minds of your audience. We've also introduced the BrainPath™ template, which is the placeholder and organizer for the stories and parables you will tell to influence your clients during business presentations. Throughout, we have reinforced the popular saying that 'facts tell, but stories sell'. Now it is time to look closer at how to actually create and deliver a business parable. The focus of this chapter will be to cover the basics of storytelling content and structure so that you have the complete tools for creating and delivering influential, persuasive presentations. Additionally, you will learn how to create the three most important parables you must have in your repertoire: the parables of *Who*, *Why*, and *How*.

WHAT IS THE PURPOSE OF A BUSINESS PARABLE?

The purpose of a business parable is to make a client benefit point, and to do so at an emotional level, where it will bring the listener closer to a decision in your favor. Parables, like stories, are invaluable in helping you:

- Gain attention.
- Connect emotionally.
- Disarm the audience.
- Produce *'Aha!'*s that help clients solve problems.

Consider the following question. Which of the following is the first thing you should do before writing a parable point?

a. Determine exactly what point you want to make.
b. Determine what parable will best help you make that point.
c. Create an outline for your presentation.
d. Consider what facts you have to support your statements.

If you picked any of the above, you may already be on the wrong path! Never start out by asking yourself "What *points* shall I make?" – because that may very easily lead you down the path of a 'ME' focused, feature-and-product-centric presentation, and your listeners will very quickly tune you out. Before you begin the process of writing a parable point, you should ask, "What *client* challenges must I address?" Remember, your business presentation should be all about, and in the service of your prospective clients, *not* you.

Think in terms of delivering *one* over-arching, persuasive theme or message, which solves a critical customer problem. Most business presentations suffer because they make lots of important little data points that together leave no single, powerful, persuasive impression on the minds of listeners. No sense of *'Aha!'* Your audience should be able to easily answer the question, "What central point was made today, and how do I benefit from it?" In order to achieve any kind of influence or viral word-of-mouth campaign from a business presentation, you must make that one clear, powerful benefit point. This could be a point about how your product works, how other customers have succeeded with your solutions, or who you are and why your audience should listen to you in the first place. Once you've decided what customer challenge you want to address, you can step back and think of interesting stories and analogies you can tell to spark their interest, and deliver that benefit point as a metaphor. The benefit point of a parable can be a premise, a theme, an argument, or simply any issue you want to highlight for your clients. Your process of creating and delivering parable points must begin by determining what issues are most important to your client, and then reverse-engineering your parables to support those points.

THE DIFFERENT TYPES OF BUSINESS PARABLES

If your goal is to influence people through business presentations, there are three basic kinds of parable points at your disposal – Parables of Who, Why, and How. The general premise for these parables is usually that something is amiss or could be better in the customer's world, and your product or service is here – at the rescue. Unlike traditional 'problem/solution' presentations with technical data and bullet-points, a parable is an indirect way of making the same points, with the added advantage that it also helps you increase the emotional impact of your presentation on listeners. The following table shows an overview of the different types of parable points:

1. Parables for establishing trust	2. Parables for establishing customer interest.	3. Parables for making client Benefit points.
Parables of Who: *Who I am – my credibility, trustworthiness, and likeability.*	Parables of Why: *Why you should listen to me or to my organization: "what's in it for the client?*	Parables of How: *How this or that feature works and provides a customer benefit.*

The first type helps you establish trust, (such as parables explaining *who* you are, and *why* your audience should listen to you). The second type helps you explain individual customer benefit points, (the parables of *how* your solutions are delivered). Any of these stories can be used to deliver the big *'Aha!'* that overarching, memorable, central point. All of these parable types have one common goal: helping you indirectly connect your clients logically and emotionally to how you and your solution can help them solve important problems.

If you were to write down the central "point" of your parable, it should ideally fit on one line of a sentence. It should be memorable, and it must be written from your client's point of view, not yours. You want to write down a point that you could imagine your clients saying to themselves as they leave the room. Your point should also be memorable enough that they will be repeating it to themselves for a long time thereafter. Some examples of what you might want your clients to say to themselves after your presentation might be:

- "That was really user-friendly!"
- "All you have to do is log on, and the rest is done for you!"
- "They actually care!"
- "They are available to me 24/7!"

This becomes your starting-place. People always connect better to things they *discover* themselves. Your task is to be their guide. Now you are ready to create the analogies that will gently lead your clients to their own discovery of this or that point – which is basically how your product or service provides them specific, measurable benefits or returns on investment.

WRITE DOWN YOUR PARABLES

Your next step in creating a powerful and persuasive business parable is to actually *write* it down! Yes, with a pen and paper. (Or computer, of course.) Most people are not aware of how carefully the greatest business storytellers toil at preparing their stories. By writing down your story, you can review it from a visual, auditory, structural, as well as an emotional point of view, and you can edit and update it many times until it is just right. Writing also helps you keep the parable short. You never want your business parable to go on for too long. Parables are shorter than stories, and they are designed to get to the point fast, while carrying a strong lesson or moral that strikes at the heart. Ideally you should keep your parables within a 100 – 300 word count maximum so that you stay under five minutes, depending on your rate of speech. (Most men speak at about 140 – 150 words per minute, while the average rate for women is about 160 wpm) If you speak at a rate of 150 wpm, a 300-word parable will take two minutes per parable – which is almost too long.   One minute is preferable. Write your story down, count the words, and keep them short and pithy. The best Parables are the shortest.

THE DEFINITION OF A PARABLE POINT

A parable point is a short narrative.

Consider the following example: imagine that your task is to persuade a group of information management specialists that your product can ensure that they will get real-time, *reliable* information to their entire global organization whenever they need to. Imagine that you have showed them bullet-point charts ad nauseam – making this same claim – but they just hadn't bought in to the idea yet. They just couldn't understand or grasp the benefit of this particular feature. So, in the parable point tradition, instead of more bullet-points, you start by telling them the following story:

In 2000, Al Gore was projected the winner of the Florida election by all three major television networks.

That was a short narrative, but it has one big problem. It makes no point! In your mind, you are probably thinking, 'So what?" This is *not* the effect you want to have on your listeners. Let's amend our definition a bit.

A parable point is a short narrative that makes a powerful point.

That's much better. First, you must determine what your point will be. In this case, our point could be that disseminating large quantities of information can be dangerous if quality and truth are not verified. Or in other words, quantity is not synonymous with quality. If we accept that this is our point, and we are proposing to the customer that our product provides the benefit of quality *and* quantity, then consider this adjustment to the story:

In 2000, Al Gore was projected the winner of the Florida election by all three major television networks. However, after a lengthy court battle, George W. Bush was eventually pronounced 43rd president of the United States, which goes to show that not verifying data before releasing it can be very dangerous.

The narrative statement has been improved because we can now infer the consequence that occurred; however, it still has a challenge. It is not yet a *story*. It has no 'hook' because it possesses neither a dramatic effect, nor a clear structure. How can we amend this? The solution lies with Aristotle, who prescribed over two thousand years ago, the idea that every good story must have a dramatic structure. His recommendation was to divide up your story into a beginning, middle, and an end. In a business presentation, the basic structural components you'll need for writing parables are the four 'C's:

1. Context   - (beginning)
2. Conflict   - (middle)
3. Change   - (middle)
4. Crux   - (the end, and *point* of the parable)

You need a *context* to set up the beginning of the story, establish the characters, and prepare your listeners for the main elements of the narrative. In traditional folktales, this is where you usually start with "once upon a time, there was a…" The next part, which is the *conflict*, usually starts with 'one-day, so and so did this . . ." After that, you then proceed to describe what happened to the subject of your story. Make sure you get into the conflict quickly. Listeners have no patience for long introductions. The conflict is where you explain what's wrong. Here you will answer the questions: What problem has to be solved? What is the source of your proposed desire to create a change? Once you've established the context and the conflict, then its time for the *change* event. This could take on many forms. In some cases, it could be a surprise, a magical revelation, a moment of truth, a piece of humor, or in the classic 'hero' tales, the point where the hero learns the truth and is now better armed to go back and win the battle. The purpose of the context and conflict sections of a parable is simply to 'set up' the story, and create expectations in the minds of your listeners. Usually, (not always), the change event serves to surprise, cause laughter, create an *'Aha!'* experience, or essentially change the assumptions a listener may have held during your setup. In essence, the change event delivers the 'punchline' of your Parable. Finally, the *crux* is where you deliver the accompanying benefit *point* of the parable - which drives your message home.

Consider this:

News organizations have traditionally done quite well forecasting and projecting who wins elections in the United States – even before official ballots have been counted.

They do this through a sophisticated system of exit polling. However, in 2000, Al Gore was projected the winner of the Florida election by all three major television networks, but this time, they were wrong!

What happened next was a lengthy court battle, and it was only after several days and hanging chads that George W. Bush was eventually pronounced 43rd president of the United States. The good news is that an important lesson had been learned. The three networks now realized that they needed better methods for checking and crosschecking their data before publishing their projections to the world.

They learned that data quantity is not synonymous with data quality.

A client listening to this short parable will be much more receptive to your point about quality vs. quantity because you have removed them from their immediate fears, realities, and expectations, and taken them to a separate place of agreement, an example they already know, where the truth of your point can stand more comfortably on its own. Not only did you get their attention by telling a story, you reached their emotions because they could all relate to the frustration of that election period. Finally, you may have even produced an *'Aha!'* in their minds because now they can see in their own terms – in their own experience – how too much data without an adequate system of reliability and verification can hurt their business. Here's a more comprehensive definition:

"A parable point is a short narrative that establishes a **context** and

conflict, introduces a **change** or resolution to the challenge, and ends with the **crux**, or business point, which leads a client to understand and buy-in to what you are trying to communicate."

DUALITY: A LESSON FROM THE SCIENCE OF HUMOR

How does this duality – this interaction between parables and points – create the magic *'Aha!'* in the human brain? How do parables, with points closely in tow, manage to get into the brain and cause a listener's emotions to become receptive, thus allowing for a greater appreciation of the benefits that a speaker is trying to convey? To understand how this occurs, it is instructive to look at the science of how jokes inspire humor. According to psychologists, the dual use of 'setup' and 'punch-line', are the magical ingredients required for producing humor. Similarly, in a business presentation, the dual use of parables and points represent the components that lead to greater understanding and emotional influence.

Freud was one of the first scholars to propose a scientific theory behind humor. Freud suggested that neural arousal in the brain, followed by a subsequent arousal-reduction, is the psychological engine behind the production of humor through jokes (Wyer & Collins, 1992). More recent scholars, such as Berlyne and Victor Raskin have confirmed this neural process. This arousal and arousal-reduction progression is caused by what is today known in the comedy world as *setup* and *punch-line*. Essentially, when a person uses a story to create neural arousal in your brain, they are setting up an expectation. To create the arousal-reduction process, they sharply diverge from the first story with a second one, usually a surprise – which we commonly refer to as the punch-line. It is the punch-line that delivers the laughter in a joke. A good way to understand the science behind how a joke works is to consider its structure. For example:

"Why did the chicken cross the road?" [*Setup*]

When you tell a joke, you are building up an expectation – a neural arousal – in the mind of your listener, up to a point where they become highly engaged. At a crucial point, you provide the answer, which delivers a surprising twist and elicits a neural arousal-reduction. In this case, our logical minds are going to be busy trying to put together an explanation for why the chicken crossed the road, by tapping into whatever stereotypes and assumptions we may have about chickens and roads. At exactly the right moment, when the mind has been sufficiently aroused, the comedian will follow with the answer, intentionally designed to contradict the assumptions, mislead, surprise, and therefore produce an immediate arousal-reduction.

"To get to the other side!" [*Punch-line*]

This sharp arousal-reduction is what produces laughter. The setup is the first section of the joke, and it arouses and prepares the mind for a pleasant surprise, while the punchline is the section of the joke that releases the tension, delivers the surprise, the '*Aha!*', and thus, the humor. One of the most important findings about humor is that it aids in memory retention over the long run. The disruption of pattern jolts the brain, and transfers the information from short-term to long-term memory. Thus, people tend to remember jokes more than regular statements. Figure 9.1 shows how comedians design jokes:

Figure 9.1. The Dual *Setup* and *Punchline* Structure of a Joke

Parables work in a similar way, except that the outcome is an '*Aha!*' experience, not laughter. In the same way that a joke has a setup and punchline, a parable has a *story* and a *benefit point*. The brain-based process of creating modern-day business parables is therefore similar to how professionals create comedy, albeit with different components and intended results:

Comedy:	Setup + Punchline = **Laughter**

Presentations;	Parable + Benefit Point = *'Aha!'*

In a presentation, first you build audience connection and interest through a parable, and then you provide them with the accompanying benefit point you are trying to convey. This creates the *'Aha!'* experience – helping your listeners become more emotionally connected to the benefits that you are proposing. Like jokes, your brain responds to the pattern shift between the story and the point, makes the association, and tends to move the information from short term to long-term memory. Certainly, clients will make more decisions in your favor if they can remember your point, and parables help them remember in ways that facts, data, and bullet-points simply cannot.

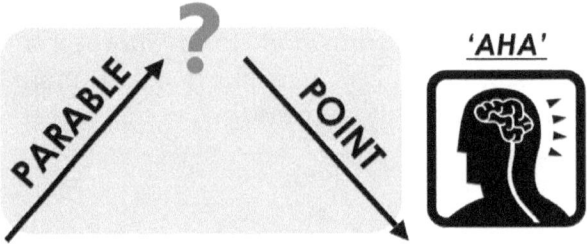

Figure 9.2. The Dual *Parable* and *Benefit Point* Structure of a Parable

WHERE DO YOU GET IDEAS FOR YOUR PARABLE POINTS?

Ideas are everywhere! In your own history of experiences, on TV, on the radio, in folktales, on the Internet, at your job, at home – the list is endless. You just have to keep your ears open for good story ideas. (Of course, it is best to give appropriate credit for the source of any information you use in a business parable). You will have to brainstorm and throw many story ideas on the table in search of the best and most powerful story to use with a certain benefit point. One of the best ways to generate parable ideas is to get together with like-minded people, family, or co-workers, and throw out story ideas that map to your benefit points. Sometimes, a great idea for a story will come from the most unexpected places.

Sometimes the best parables come from the experience of other people. One of my favorite parables came from a workshop I attended. My mentor, Les Brown, told the story of a dog that wouldn't stop moaning and groaning. The point of his parable was that people can become complacent when things don't hurt badly enough. I took that story, and, (always explaining the original source), modified it for my business audiences. I still use the dog, but I tell the story in support my concept of a formula for influence in business environments, and it has always been a hit with my listeners. When I am done, they always get the message: Help your clients make a change! Raise their levels of emotion! Get them excited about the positive benefits that are ahead of them – if they make that change!

THE ANCIENT USE OF PARABLES

Dr. David Dorsey, in his book, *The Literary Structure of the Old Testament*, suggests that ancient Hebrew writers and teachers used literary conventions that were vastly different from ours. One of the most popular of those conventions was *parallelism* (Dorsey, 1999), which was the preferred teaching methodology used by Jesus during his lifetime. This teaching device, also known as the *mashal-nimshal*, refers to the pairing of allegory and explanation as a means of teaching. Mashal is a Hebrew word for metaphor or 'parable', while Nimshal means the accompanying explanation, or 'point'.

Parallelism was the preferred and most effective way for communicating a point of view in such a way that listeners would more readily accept it. Author Jeffrey L. Curry built on Dorsey's work to propose that Jesus habitually used the power of parables and their accompanying points (or 'real-life targets,' as he calls them) for explaining his core messages, and indeed, as a way of recruiting disciples:

In the mind of the author of a parable, there must reside a purpose for creating it. The reason for creating the parable is what I call its "real-life target." This real-life target, in the mind of the author, is a situation that needs further illumination, or a concrete and firm understanding. So the teacher, because he wants to teach his students about this real-life target, begins to create a fictitious story, usually a simple story, sometimes even one sentence that would illustrate the lesson he wishes to teach. This is the parable. It is a mysterious and allusive tale told with a hidden emphasis. The parable, properly employed, is designed to lay hold of the student; to capture him and to make him ask questions. Then, after the parable has laid hold of the student, the teacher will reveal its intended target. Once the student has been given the parable and its real-life target, the student has within his hands, the tools for understanding, and the tools for learning what the master has wrought to teach. (Curry, 2004, p. 19)

Two thousand years ago, Jesus knew that people don't hear or see as well with their minds, as with their emotions – a concept that is now scientifically validated. As a result of this simple truth, he also knew that he had to speak in a language that his listeners understood – using metaphors from their everyday lives to convey unorthodox, complex new information to virgin listeners. He knew that his message had to be repeated (virally) by disciples and followers even after he was gone. To achieve his goal of getting a multitude of people to buy into his message, his medium of choice, his code, if you will - was parables.

The use of parables as a parallel device for explaining complex subjects still works today. People still think and understand things better in metaphor and pictures than through raw, concrete facts. As the saying goes, 'if a picture is worth a thousand words, then a parable is worth a thousand pictures." If you have a difficult feature or benefit to explain, convert it into a parable and an accompanying benefit point. Remember that in business, as we suggested earlier, your stories must be *true*, or else, they will not be meaningful as representations of your facts, features, and benefits. The business parable as a communication device allows you to get deeper and more naturally into the minds of your listeners, so that they can more readily understand your accompanying benefit points.

THE PARABLE OF 'WHO'

Once upon a time there was a business executive who showed up five minutes late for his presentation. As he rushed into the boardroom, he could almost feel the heat from the unforgiving, staring eyes that burned into him. He apologized profusely and quickly jumped into his business presentation as gracefully as he possibly could. He was even able to earn some laughter by blaming his tardiness on the strange string of events that had happened since he had woken up that morning. No one said a word throughout his presentation. At the end of it, he proudly felt he had achieved his objective, salvaged his job, his reputation, and even the speech itself. He concluded by asking the popular business presentation end-game question, "Any questions?" Someone stood up and asked, "Who are you again?" That was when he finally realized that he had inadvertently walked into the wrong boardroom!

This short parable showcases the importance of letting people know upfront who you are and why they should listen to you. If you don't, they will tune you out. This particular problem can be fixed by telling a simple story about who you are – a story called the 'Parable of Who' – the first in the triad of essential parables.

The first thing you must establish in a business presentation is who you are and why your audience should listen to you. As we discussed earlier, credibility and trust are the first things on the minds of your listeners. Instead of bullet-points that tersely state that you are the manager of this or that company, tell your audience a well-packaged, interesting story about yourself that doubles up as a way of preparing them for the influential, benefit-laden discussion you are about to lead them through.

> "If you want to know me, then you must know my story, for my story defines who I am."
>
> - Dan McAdams

Your identity as a professional must always be explained to others from your client's point of view, not yours. The same is true for the stories you tell to drive home the point of what you do. For example, when people begin presentations they usually talk about who they are using bullet-points that assert the following:

- My name.
- My title.

- My achievements.
- My process.

Notice a pattern here? The main problem with all of these bullet-points is that they don't start from the customer's viewpoint. The same exact points could be made more persuasive if they were conveyed in the form of a client-centered parable of 'who'. To create your parable of 'who', start by listing the objectives of the story you're going to tell – but this time, from the client's point of view:

- My name and how I help my clients.
- An example of the client problems I've solved.
- A story that shows I understand the client's challenges.

These three new objectives will resonate much more with an audience, and will be more effective if you weave them all into a nicely crafted parable. As we discussed in chapter 9, every parable should have a dramatic structure. The easiest way to build a dramatic story is to use the four 'C's – context, conflict, change, conclusion. In the Parable of Who, of which you are the subject, you have to establish a context, show a conflict that you've had to deal with, explain the change event, and conclude with your benefit points. Throughout this process, you want to ensure that you hit the objectives you laid out for your parable. Here's a rough example of my parable of 'who', as I would present it in one of my business presentation skills workshops:

MY PARABLE OF 'WHO'

"My name is Pelè Raymond, and I help professionals win more clients through business presentations – even if they struggle with public speaking.

For many years I was in corporate sales and marketing. My job was to travel the globe and deliver business presentations that evangelized our products. I realized that most of our company's presentations were canned, bullet-point affairs that usually bored our clients. We were losing money and wasting organizational resources because our client conversion rates were abysmal, and I soon realized that I had to do something about the situation or risk losing my job.

One day, I decided to do something dramatic. I threw out my bullet-point slides and started telling stories and parables instead – indirect metaphors that explained my points. I started engaging my audience by asking them questions during my presentations so that they could tell me their stories. I noticed a sharp increase in my client conversion rates. Not only did I save my job and benefit financially, I also discovered the secret thing that all customers love, which also happens to be a passion in my life: storytelling!

So I started reading all the books I could on storytelling, speaking, persuasion, influence and so on, and sure enough, I found that the one common theme in trying to influence people was the ability to tell a good story. I went back to school and got a PhD in business, and later joined Toastmasters, where I became an award-winning speaker. I then put all my knowledge, research, and experience into creating the parable point presentation system you are about to learn today. So far, practically every one of my clients have seen an increase in their client conversion rates as a result of these training seminars and workshops."

(298 words)

Can you see how this short story would be more effective than the standard "who I am" bullet-point slide? Did you notice the dramatic structures of context, conflict, change, and conclusion? Did you notice how I also set up my audience for the system they are about to receive? Your story should engage your target audience, describe you in a language they understand, showcase an understanding of their challenges, and show them the potential benefits of working with you. Throughout, you'll help them get to know you better, increase their trust and comfort-level, and become more receptive to your coming presentation.

THE PARABLE OF 'WHY'

Telling your clients who you are is very important, but equally important is that you establish early on why they should listen to you. You may have made that point somewhere in your parable of who, but you may not have fully answered one of their most burning questions:

Why are you any different than anyone else?

The answer to this question is really your unique competitive advantage, or as some may say, your unique selling proposition. This is the 'why you', or 'why your company' question. Once again, instead of rolling out bullet-points, tell a parable that makes a point. There are many ways to differentiate yourself. Your organization may already have a canned differentiation point, or you may have to take some of the following approaches:

- A unique approach to providing solutions.
- A specific market niche.
- Testimonials from satisfied clients.
- A satisfaction guarantee.

Your task is to take these points, and roll them into a nicely packaged, interesting story. One of my favorite parables of 'why' comes from life coach and motivational speaker Tony Robbins. His unique competitive advantage appears to be the following:

- He's read every book on the planet about self-improvement.
- For 30 years, I've presented a formula that works for millions.
- My formula is what turned me from an over-weight, broke young man, into the success story you see today.

Basically, at every opportunity, Tony reminds you that he is credible, his solution works, and that he has walked the talk in his own life. He presents himself as a model for his clients, and he does this by sharing his parable of 'why' at the beginning of every seminar.

In order to write a great parable of 'why', as always, make sure that your story has a set of objectives, a dramatic structure, and answers the question of 'what makes you different'. Remember, however, that what makes you different has to have meaning and a benefit for your clients, and cannot just be something of general interest about you. Your parable of why is what earns you the right to speak. While your parable of who deals with trust and comfort-levels in the presentation itself, this is all about why anyone should spend their valuable time listening to you and your presentation in the first place.

THE PARABLE OF 'HOW'

Sir Francis Bacon once said, 'By far the best proof is experience." Throughout your business presentations, you will need to provide examples and proof of the points you are making. Once again, just telling people that your solution can do this or that is never as powerful as showing them how it actually did it through a story. As the popular saying goes, 'the proof is in the pudding'. If you are able to create and deliver short stories that show examples and proof of your features and benefits, you will go a long way in persuading listeners to see your point of view.

One of the biggest problems in business presentations is that they make statements, but fail to provide any proof. The purpose of the parable of 'how' is to address how you are able to do what you say you do. As they say in the state of Missouri – "Show me!" The parable of 'how' is also the most commonly used parable because it is essentially how you communicate your various features and benefit points. A form of proof must accompany every single client benefit that you discuss, and in many cases, a story is the perfect, most disarming way of showing proof. However, you don't always have to tell a story. Sometimes a demonstration, or an interactive audience exercise will serve the same purpose. The point is that you must actually craft and rehearse this parable just like any other, and make sure that it is focused on the client, not on you.

One of my favorite examples of a 'parable of how' is a small, interactive parable-game I developed for explaining that my company's competitive advantage was our pre-packaged, ready to use, turnkey approach. Instead of just saying that we had pre-built components in our offering, I would go through the following 'Parable of How'.

MY PARABLE OF 'HOW'

Once upon a time, there were two companies. One installed a complicated, overly feature-laden product that was difficult to implement and use, while the other company subscribed to an online product with pre-packaged components in easy-to-understand user fields that were delivered so that no installation was necessary. Fast-forward two years, and the first company with the sophisticated solution went out of business while the second company with the online, easy-to-use solution had not only recouped its ROI, but showed clear profit margins. Why do you think one achieved such great success while the other failed miserably?

Let me show you how. May I have two volunteers, please?

(At this point, two people come up, and I give each of them a closed box containing identical Mickey Mouse puzzles. One of the boxes has twenty pieces, while the other has some of the pieces attached together so that the puzzle appears to have only five combined pieces.)

I then say: "Ready get set, go" – and the two contestants open their boxes and start putting the puzzle together. Of course, the volunteer with the pre-packaged puzzle wins each time. We play with this a few times just to get more people enjoying the interaction.

Once I reveal to the audience why one solution works so much better, I display a PowerPoint® slide that shows a picture of the two puzzles, and I explain to them that our product is superior in the market place because we make things much simpler for our users. By prepackaging known user needs into simpler routines, we deliver ease-of-use, so they never have to waste time trying to figure things out.

Our benefit? We do the heavy lifting behind the scenes so you can focus on what matters – running your company!

(296 Words)

PUTTING IT ALL TOGETHER

So far we have laid out the various parables that you can use to answer the questions in your clients' brains, such as:

"Who are you?"
"Why should we listen to you?"
"How does your solution really work?"

There are many more stories and parables that you will need to develop as part of your campaign of business storytelling and influence, but the rule of thumb remains the same: instead of bullet-points and technical jargon, tell a story, and make a point.

Tell a parable, make a point!

Business storytelling is the core technology that powers the parable point presentation system, and it is something anyone can learn to do, regardless of their comfort level with public speaking. Remember that clients – like all people – feel first, before they can think. No matter how technical your information is, it must be understood both logically and emotionally. Help your clients get to 'Aha!' by taking them through the magical land of stories, and dropping them off right at the doorstep of your business points. Tell a parable, make a point, and you will find yourself winning more clients than you can handle – even if you hate public speaking.

EXERCISE

The following template is a set of questions that you will answer as part of creating your Parables;

- What type of parable am I going to write? Who, Why, How?

- What are the main objectives of this parable?

- Is it clearly divided into the four C's of context, conflict, change, and conclusion?

- Do I have a clear 'setup and punchline?'

- Where can I get ideas?

- How will I rehearse?

10. The QueryTalk™ Storytelling Template

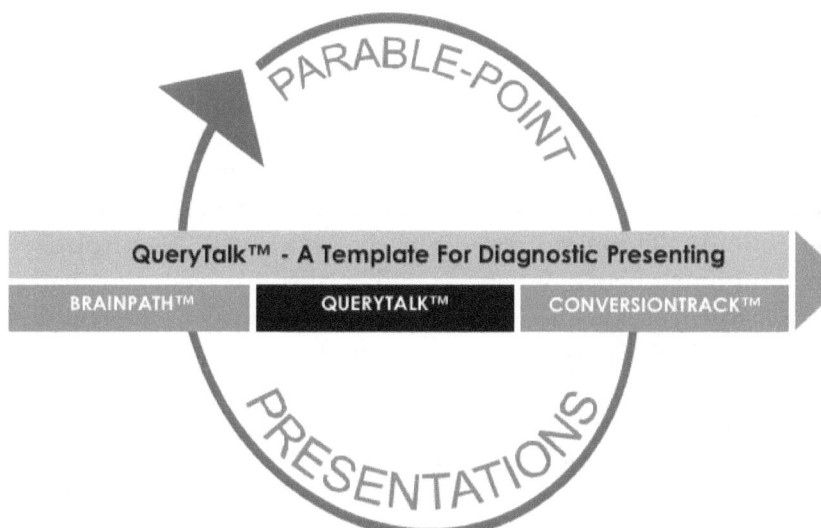

"The art of teaching is the art of assisting discovery."
- MARK VAN DOREN

So far, we have described the storyboarding and multimedia creation tasks in preparing a parable point presentation. You have also reviewed the process of writing and delivering your own business parables. Now it is time to rehearse and deliver the presentation. Remember we discussed the idea that the second biggest mistake that sales presenters make is that they hold on too tightly to their tools, such as PowerPoint and bullet-points? Remember "death by PowerPoint?" Well, the antidote to death by PowerPoint is to deliver *Parable Points* through a process called QueryTalk™. This is an *interactive* approach to communicating with clients in business presentations, and it represents the main performance feature of the parable point presentation system. Instead of delivering one-way, bullet-point slideshows, you must learn to walk away you're your tools and practice a communication style that involves your audience talking with you or performing activities at least 30% of the time!

"The only kind of learning which significantly influences behavior is self-discovered or self-appropriated learning - truth that has been assimilated in experience."   - Carl Rogers

Get your clients involved in the process! The key to the QueryTalk process is to ask Socratic questions and give your audience things to do as part of your presentation. What this does, (similar to a workshop environment), is get them to participate more fully in what you are talking about. Through participation, they will internalize your information much better. When the audience is involved, and shares the discussion with you, they are much more highly engaged, and will, as Carl Rogers stated, 'self-discover' the points and concepts you are trying to make. A more involved client will better appreciate your product, understand your competitive advantages, and will be more likely to use your product or retain your services.

During business presentations, what is your ratio of talking versus asking questions? 70/30? 50/50? 40/60? Here is a rough breakdown of the percentage of time you should allocate between yourself and the audience in the QueryTalk process.

Focus	Description	Time
YOU & YOUR MULTIMEDIA	Speaking, asking questions, telling stories, showing pictures.	70%
AUDIENCE	Telling you their stories, or doing exercises and games designed to explain your points.	**_30%_**

QueryTalk is actually a compound word. 'Query' suggests that you should ask probing questions to elucidate and clarify your client's needs and values during the discussion. The second part is the acronym 'T.A.L.K.', which refers to Touch, Action, Laughter, and Knowledge. Here's an explanation of each term:

- **Query** – Talk through questions, (with a clear vision of the lessons or points you want them to learn through your questioning), and seek audience involvement throughout the presentation. Make direct eye contact with the listeners and continually search for opportunities to get someone to respond to you with a story, question, or comment.

In addition to asking questions to get them talking to you, your goal is to make sure you continually verify, confirm, and 'diagnose' the clients' needs in real time. *Expose the pain!* All the research you have done about your client is useless if it proves to be wrong, or if they aren't made to feel the pain or urgency during your discussion. It is better to continue verifying than to position yourself as knowing all things. (Although you do need to demonstrate that you cared enough to do legitimate research, but don't completely ignore the experts you have in front of you. They know their problems better than you ever could.)

Use questions to drive deeper into the formula for influence (I = E + A). By asking questions, you can elicit an increase in the positive and negative emotions that work together to create influence. According to renowned educator R. W. Paul (1984), here are the different kinds of Socratic questions you can use in a presentation:

- Questions for clarification
- Questions that probe assumptions
- Questions that probe reasons
- Questions about viewpoints and perspectives
- Questions that probe implications and consequences
- Questions that make your point

- **T** – *Touch* your audience emotionally. Make sure that there are pieces of your delivery that address the human element – people's real needs are not always directly related to business, and the cold, impersonal walls of an organization. People care about their families, their hopes and aspirations, friendships, and other 'soft' topics. Don't ignore these kinds of issues even as you discuss very technical business subjects. By bringing your speech down to a human level, you will connect emotionally with people, and increase your chances of getting through to them.

- **A** – *Action* is very important in speaking. Remember Albert Mehrabian's 7/38/55 rule, which states that people understand what you say largely from your non-verbal communication signals. Words only account for 7% of the meaning that you communicate. How you say your words vocally is responsible for 38%, and your facial expressions and body language account for a whopping 55% of what your audience understands! Becoming good at QueryTalk means that you will pay attention not only to what your words are saying, but also to how you say things, what emphasis you place, and how you move your body while you are communicating.

The other part of 'action' is using games or other interactive activities to get your audience to learn collaboratively with each other. Games are a powerful way of demonstrating points, and they work simply because people 'get' things better through experiential learning. If you can design interactive games or demonstrations that involve the audience, you will go a long way in getting them to understand and remember your points.

- **L** – *Laughter* is an important part of any presentation. It calms people down, opens them up mentally, disarms, them, and makes them care more about you and what you have to say. Essentially, people like you more when they laugh with you. Even if your intention is not to be a comedian, do not ever miss an opportunity to write in a funny statement here and there because this is sure to keep your audience continually interested in what you are saying – and it keeps them awake too! The reason laughter is instrumental in enhancing your presentations, is related to how your brain works. Laughter disinhibits the reptilian brain and allows information to flow more easily up the BrainPath. The setup of a joke gets your brain expecting one pattern to continue, and the punchline disrupts it. This disruption helps to transfer the meaning of the joke or point being made from short-term memory into long-term memory, because our brains are quick to recognize *and remember* when patterns are broken. (More on this in chapter 9 – How To Write And Deliver Business Parables). Laughter makes people pay more attention to you, and also, it helps people remember your points. If you want people to remember something, make them comfortable, and make them laugh.

- **K** – *Knowledge* is the key to creating influence. I don't mean knowledge in terms of your product's features and benefits. What I mean here is that you should help your audience think deeply about something that is important in *their* lives. Give them some new knowledge to take away which will leave them thinking long after your presentation is over. It could be a wise saying, proverb, advice, story, experience etc. Whatever it is, it must make them think, feel, and remember you, your company, or the main points of your presentation.

  Also, you want to pass on knowledge that will help build your case for influence. As Robert Cialdini identified, the six principles of influence (liking, reciprocity, social proof, consistency, authority and scarcity), can only work if you inject your audience with the right knowledge that will act as an agent for these six kinds of influence. Your goal is to give them reasons for why they should like you, reciprocate, or pay attention to social proof when it comes to you and your product.

BUILDING YOUR QUERYTALK CONTENT

Now that you have designed the overall flow of your presentation, you need to focus on how you will deliver it. QueryT.A.L.K.™ is the process of speaking through questions that continuously encourage your clients to tell you their stories and become an integral part of the communication process.

Query
Remember – The best business presentations are 100% about the client. What specific questions will you ask your listeners in order to make sure they are sharing their stories and challenges during your presentation, and that your discussion is interactive and diagnostic?

List your Top Ten 'QueryTALK' Questions:

1. _____

2. _____

3. _____

4. _____

5. _____

6. _____

7. _____

8. _____

9. _____

10. _____

T. (Touch)

How will you touch your audience emotionally? What parables will you use?

A. (Action)

What will you ask your audience to do physically during the presentation? How will they participate? How will you use your own body language to convey certain points?

L. (Laughter)

What specific humor, jokes, or stories will you use to lighten up your audience?

K. (Knowledge)

What profound knowledge and insights will you impart on this audience that is emotionally meaningful to them?

Use the QueryTalk template in Figure 10.1 to fill in your content.

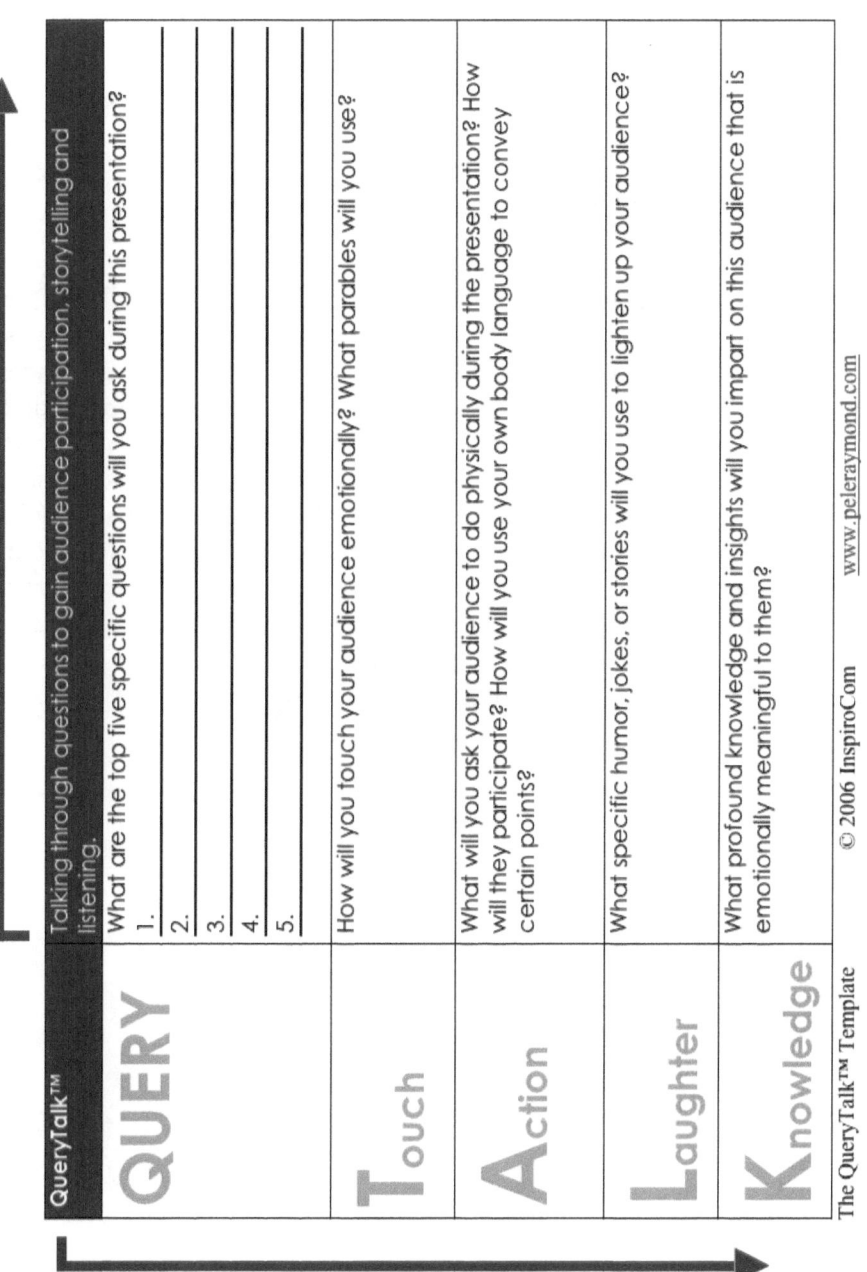

Figure 10.1. The QueryTalk™ Template For Delivering Presentations

Most good salespeople understand and practice the power of relationship selling. Building trust, rapport, and getting the prospect involved...

What is sorely needed however, is **relationship presenting!**

What if your listeners are resistant, and don't want to tell you their stories? How do you encourage them to open up? The best strategy is to build this expectation for the group up front. Show them, by reaching out to them, that your presentation style depends on audience participation. Explain to them upfront that you believe the only way they will maximize the day's discussion is if they get involved, ask questions, share their experiences, and tell their stories. Remind them that they have a vested interest in the outcome of this discussion. (Don't ask them to reserve questions till the end like most presenters do). This way, everyone is involved, no one will fall asleep on you, and you will have an audience that is ready to take action on things because they participated fully. They were actively a part of the discussion!

SOLUTION **3** : CONVERSIONTRACK

The 3 Big Mistakes	The 3 Big Solutions
1. The **'ME'** Mindset	BrainPath™ Storyboarding
2. One-Way **bullet-point** slides	QueryTalk™ Storytelling
3. No **system** for improvement	ConversionTrack™

Congratulations! You have now learned the process of creating, (BrainPath™), and delivering (QueryTalk™) your parable point presentations. Now the question is, "How do you prepare, practice, perfect, and improve your presentations? Well, the answer is to test and measure them, because you cannot improve what you cannot measure. In solution 3, you will be introduced to:

- A system for continually testing, measuring, and improving your presentations.
- An exponential system for increasing conversion rates.
- A parable point presentation workbook to get you started right away on your next business presentation.

11. How To Increase Your Client Conversion Rates

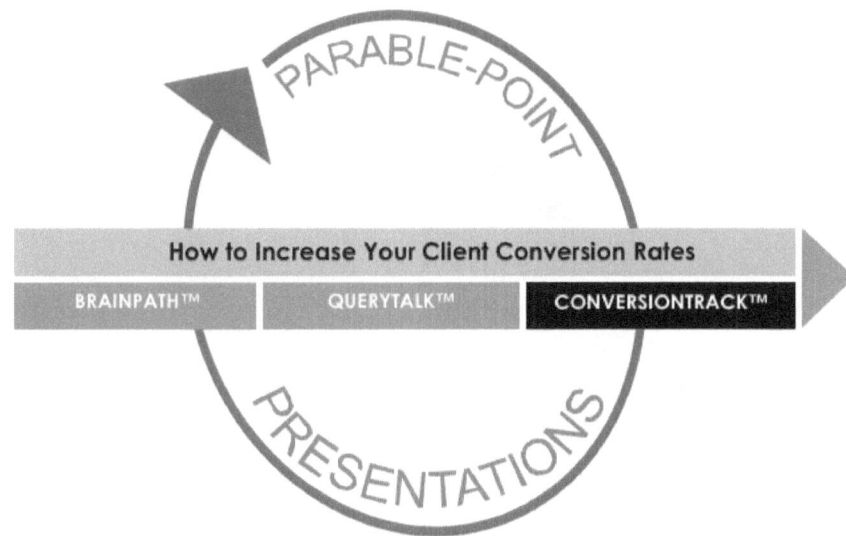

"Practice is the best of all instructors."
                        - PUBLILIUS SYRUS

In the early 20th century, advertising pioneer Claude C. Hopkins made a bold assertion: that advertising could and should be practiced as a science. He was advocating the use of testing and measuring as a more accurate way to improve the results of ad campaigns. In his seminal book: *Scientific Advertising*, he likened all past advertising to blind trial and error:

> It was like a man trying to build a modern locomotive without first ascertaining what others had done. It was like a Columbus starting out to find an undiscovered land …They rarely arrived at their port. When they did - by accident - it was by a long roundabout course. (Hopkins, 1923, p. 217)

Hopkins' point is well taken and practiced by advertisers, marketers, and sales people today. In essence, he was making the claim that opinions about the effectiveness of marketing communications are not nearly as useful as finding out what actual customers think or feel based on their statements or actions. Here is Hopkins' opinion on the importance of testing and measuring:

> Almost any question can be answered, cheaply, quickly, and finally, by a test campaign. And that's the way to answer them – not by arguments around a table. Go to the court of last resort – the buyers of your product. (Hopkins, 1923, p. 294)

Sounds logical, right? Absolutely! Yet amazingly, most people don't realize that business presentations are akin to a microcosm of their larger marketing communications, advertising, and sales processes. As a result, they rarely test and measure the results of their presentations. If testing and measuring is good for your advertising, sales, marketing and management processes, it is certainly good for your business presentations.

Here are some reasons to test and measure your business presentations by tracking client feedback and post-presentation actions:

1. You can manage better what you can measure.
2. You can improve continuously if you track your progress.
3. You can find out what presentation strategies are working, and focus more on them.
4. You can eliminate what strategies aren't working.
5. You can get a clear picture of your client conversion rate, so that you know where and how to improve.
6. You can reduce your costs and sales cycles by knowing where to invest more or less energy, time, and money.
7. Etc., etc. – the advantages are numerous!

The way to increase your client conversion rates is through rigorous practice, testing, and measuring. You cannot improve what you cannot measure.

A SYSTEM FOR IMPROVING YOUR PRESENTATIONS

One of my favorite games at the end of a LeaderPractice full-day presentation-training workshop is when I ask each of the participants to tell the rest of us the most important thing they learned during the day. Once each person tells us how much this or that point has changed the way they will do business presentations from now on, I always follow with the question: "So what will you do tomorrow morning at 9am to implement these fantastic new business presentation skills you've just learned?" The answer I get is usually a telling smile. The participants usually know deep inside that they really had no plan for implementation. Like most people, they come to seminars, learn a great deal, and then forget them and return to their comfort-zones. I always make sure to drive home the important point that the only way to improve your presentations is to *practice*, because frankly:

> **"You can't learn to play soccer at a seminar!"**

There is a huge chasm between knowledge and results, and the only way to implement what you've learned is through continuous conditioning and practice *after* the seminar! What you need is a system and a safe environment to practice and implement the new skills you have acquired. This is what I call the *Parable Point Club*™. You can think of it as a kind of Toastmasters on steroids for the business world, and I am your business presentation coach. The Parable Point Club's rehearsal and continuous improvement system is at the heart of the ConversionTrack process.

ConversionTrack™ is the answer to the fact that most sales professionals have no clear system for continuously improving their business presentations. You may have heard the statistic that most executives spend about 90% of their time communicating, and only 1% of their time preparing to communicate. This miniscule focus on preparation is certainly not an effective way to improve. In fact, one of the most glaring mistakes sales presenters make is not practicing or critiquing themselves in any way prior to important presentations. ConversionTrack takes you back to the fundamentals: practice makes perfect, and testing and measuring each business presentation to improve performance. The ConversionTrack process involves two components:

1. Rehearsals and feedback in a Parable Point Club™
2. Measuring actual Client feedback and Conversion Rates

As Hopkins asks, how can one improve without practicing, testing, and measuring results? If you want to increase your client conversion rate, you must first know what that conversion rate is. Whenever I ask professionals what their presentation conversion rates are, they almost always provide more of an optimistic assessment than what it really turns out to be.

> "86% of executives/managers rate themselves as effective communicators. Only 17% of their audiences agreed."
>
> (Clarke & Crossland, 2002)

REHEARSALS AND FEEDBACK IN A PARABLE POINT CLUB™

The value of practice and preparation before each presentation cannot be overemphasized. Yet many sales presenters have become accustomed to just *winging* it. You really have to prepare for each presentation to make sure you are uniquely addressing the needs of the specific client you are visiting. One of the best ways to do this is to either practice in from of people, or record the main components of your presentation via video and critique yourself. By far the more effective method for effective rehearsal is to present and record yourself in front of real people – such as in role-playing groups with colleagues. You may have heard of Toastmasters, which is committed to providing exactly this kind of rehearsal and evaluation environment to help you improve public speaking ability. I recommend you create a similar environment in your organization, where you are able to get together with peers on a regular basis to rehearse and evaluate each other. Some people may suggest joining a Toastmasters club, and that is certainly a good start. While I fully endorse such an idea for improving your public speaking, it doesn't do much for improving your sales-related business presentations. When you get together with colleagues, you can focus on relevant, sales-related business topics and subject matter, and give each other feedback regarding how influential your presentations come across. At LeaderPractice, we call this the Parable Point Club™, a safe environment for testing, measuring, and improving the effectiveness of your business presentations.

MEASURING CONVERSION RATES

Now that you have a strategy for testing your presentations, let's step back and take a look at the overall process of converting clients from one phase in the buying process to another. There are essentially four variables that you can measure and influence in the overall process of winning clients, and business presentations can play a pivotal role in each one of them:

Phase in the Selling Process	Variable you can Influence?
Number of Prospecting Presentations	YES
Conversion rate from prospects to clients	(Conversion Rate is the Number of Presentations ÷ Number of clients converted).
Number of clients converted	YES
Number of purchases	YES
Overall Cost of each purchase	YES

In B2B sales situations, a single business presentation is rarely intended to 'close' the final deal. Rather, each presentation is intended to advance the sale from one step in the buying process to the next. If your business presentation produces no advancement in your overall sales campaign, then it has simply been a form of information or entertainment, and has not been effective in influencing your prospective clients. Your goal is to move your clients from one stage of the buying process to the next, ever closer to a final decision. The selling phases above involve turning *suspects* into *prospects*, and then in turn, converting them into *clients*. Once you have clients, you may deliver additional presentations to help them decide the *number* of product units to purchase, and at what *overall cost*.

Turning suspects into *prospects* is something that you can do by hosting a seminar, or providing in-house training or information sessions for the leads or referrals you have. In my days as a corporate product 'evangelist', I did a fair share of these types of presentations at trade shows, seminars, breakout sessions, or in different departments of existing clients.

Converting prospects into clients is the main goal of a business presentation. Your *conversion rate* is essentially the percentage of prospects who bought whatever you were selling, vis-à-vis those who didn't. For example, if 10 people attended a session and 3 bought your product, your conversion rate is 30% (3 ÷ 10). Or it would be 25% if you presented at 20 companies and 5 of them purchased. This is a powerful performance indicator, and it still amazes me how many people never track or measure it. The best way to ensure that you *never* improve your client conversion rate from presentations is to never know what your rate actually is.

The *number of clients converted* is exactly that: how many clients you now have as a result of your business presentations. This number does not include how many clients you have acquired from other marketing activities such as advertising or referrals. This number is solely about the number of clients converted as a result of your business presentations.

The number of *purchases per client* is a measure of how much your client bought. If you were in the enterprise software world, you would talk in terms of 'seats' – i.e. the number of software seats a company purchased.

The *dollar size of each purchase* represents how much each client paid each time they purchased your product.

WHAT IF YOU COULD INCREASE YOUR CONVERSION RATE?

Now, let's take a mathematical look at what would happen if you were able to increase some of these measurable variables by just 10%. Assume that you will do this by improving the outcome of your business presentations in each variable (shaded) phase of the process. Also assume that the following table represents the numbers you tracked in one year, and that you did the *exact* same number of presentations in the second year.

Sales Phase	Year 1	10% Increase	Result
No. of Prospect Presentations	30	30 (same as yr 1)	
Conversion Rate	33%	36.6%	
No. of Clients	10	11	
No. of Purchases	4	4.4	
Overall Cost of each Purchase	$1,000	$1,100	
Gross Revenue to your company	$40,000	**$53,240**	33%

Notice the power of exponential math. Take a look at the gross revenue to your company in the second year after a 10% increase all the way down. In the first year column, with no improvement in your business presentations, you have $40,000 – which you expected. However, after a 10% increase, (by improving business presentations in each of the three shaded phases), instead of $40,000, (which would have been an equivalent 10% increase), you now have $53,240 – a whopping 33% increase in gross revenue! That's the power of exponential math!

A **10% improvement** in your business presentations – targeted at specific phases of your sales and marketing process – creates a whopping **33% increase in revenue!**

Now, what if you could double your presentation results, such that you have a 100% increase at each presentation phase? This is certainly possible. It just means that you want to aim to double your results. If, for example, you started out with only two companies buying out of eight presentations, you now want to get four companies to buy. Let's take a look at what a 100% increase looks like:

Sales Phase	Year 1	100% Increase	Result
No. of Prospect Presentations	30	30 (same as yr 1)	
Conversion Rate	33%	66%	
No. of Clients	10	20	
No. of Purchases	4	8	
Overall Cost of each Purchase	$1,000	$2,000	
Gross Revenue to your company	$40,000	**$320,000**	**700%**

With a **100% increase** in effectiveness, achieved by improving your business presentations in each phase of the process, you could end up with $320,000 – an amazing **700% increase in revenue!**

700% may seem extraordinarily high, but mathematics does not lie: testing and measuring your business presentations can make an incredible difference, even if all it does is help you keep a scorecard of client feedback and purchases so that you know where you are, and how to improve in order to more deliberately increase your performance. By increasing your presentation effectiveness, you can go a long way toward improving your bottom line. But if you never tested or measured, you would not know where to focus your efforts, or even how to improve them.

AUDIENCE FEEDBACK HELPS BETTER TARGET YOUR EFFORTS

The ConversionTrack process is primarily built around the actual conversion numbers you track in your various presenting phases, but it is equally important to track and study how each meeting actually went. Two ways of doing this are (1) recording each presentation, or (2) collecting audience feedback after each presentation.

Sometimes it is useful to actually record an audio of your entire presentation so that you can listen to it later and assess your performance. You can do this by simply bringing in a small digital audio recorder. It is incredibly useful to review whether or not you involved your audience adequately, and to study the kinds of questions they asked or the answers they gave to the questions you asked. Overall, recording your presentation can produce valuable post-presentation information for later review and analysis.

At the end of each presentation, it may also be helpful to reserve at least five minutes to either ask questions or pass out a (very) short feedback form that collects audience feedback answers to questions such as these:

1. Are there any questions I can help you find answers to?
2. Was the presentation helpful in clarifying our business fit?
3. Did I credibly address your business challenges and needs?
4. Did you feel like you participated?
5. What were the three most important things you learned?
6. Did you experience an 'Aha!' – If so, in what area?
7. How will you use what you gained in this presentation?
8. Will you explain what you learned to others?
9. Would you like to learn more? Shall I contact you by email?
10. How can I improve this presentation to better meet your needs?

You are the best – and only – judge of when it is best to use a feedback form. Simple verbal questions and responses at the end of a presentation may suffice. Every sales situation and business presentation is different, but overall, a good feedback process should put your audience into a certain frame of mind regarding your respectful determination to satisfy their needs and address their concerns. Answers to these kinds of questions can also help you to improve your business presentations based on suggestions from the final arbiter of your effectiveness – your audience!

EXERCISE

- Do you know your Client Conversion Rate from your business presentations? Have you ever documented and tracked this crucial performance indicator?

- Go back through your records over the past three months, and write down how many clients purchased something, or were persuaded to take a specific action by your business presentations. After that, write down how many business presentations you gave to prospects in that same period of time. Next, divide the number of clients you converted by the number of presentations you gave, and multiply by 100. This is your business presentation Client Conversion Rate – a crucial number – and it will form the basis upon which you must begin to improve your results.

- Create a client feedback form that collects important information after each presentation, which will help you improve your performance.

12. The Parable Point Presentation Workbook

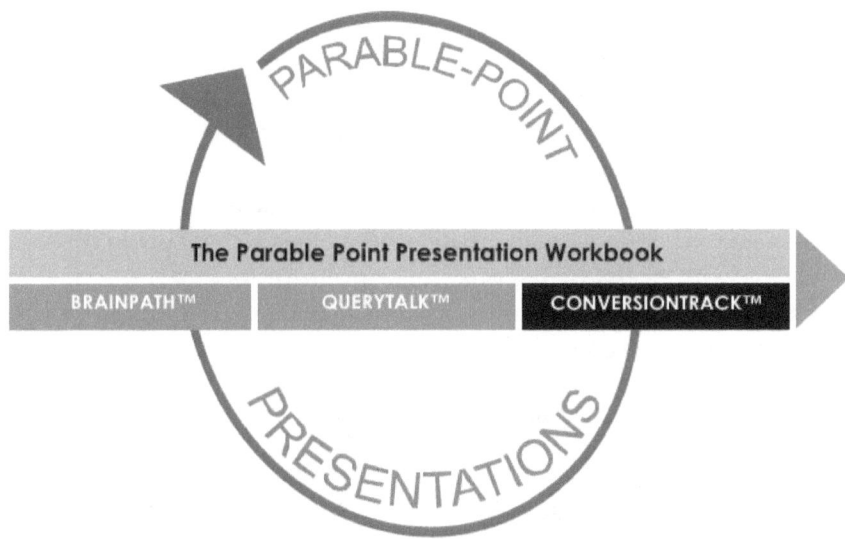

"ARE YOUR PRESENTATIONS WINNING ENOUGH CLIENTS?"

A s a professional involved in complex business to business sales, the answer to this question is the key difference between success and failure. Answering this question is extremely important, and not addressing it could be devastating – in fact, not addressing this question is the surest, and most guaranteed way to fail in your business and sales campaigns.

THE CHALLENGE OF THE MISSION-CRITICAL PRESENTATION

Imagine that you have just landed an important presentation with a major account. You should congratulate yourself for getting this far in your sales cycle. Over the past few months you've done a lot of research, conducted meetings, and built relationships within this client organization. Finally, you've been given an opportunity to speak with many, if not all of the major decision makers in this particular meeting. Top sales professionals know that this is the make-or-break moment for their entire sales campaign, and that thousands, or sometimes millions of dollars could be on the line. This is the capstone moment for all the travel, phone calls, networking and strategizing you've been doing since you began pursuing this lead! Getting this business presentation right will determine if you can move the client to the next stage in your sales process – the order! Top sales professionals know that this is no time to bore clients with hours of tedious bullet-point presentations. They know that if they fail to influence these decision makers, the entire campaign could come to a screeching halt!

THE BRIGHT SIDE

The good news is that there is a process that can be learned, practiced and implemented which will help you win more clients reliably in crucial presentations such as this one. Business presentations can become the most fruitful and rewarding part of your entire sales campaign if you master a field-proven system for conducting them. This Parable Point Presentation Workbook section is designed to help you create and deliver business presentations that will have your clients saying:

"Aha! Now I get it!"
"Can you come back and share more of this with…"
"When can we get started?"

A SEVEN-STEP SYSTEM THAT WORKS

There are three major reasons why many sales professionals don't win as many clients as they would like through business presentations:

1. They display a 'ME' mindset and don't connect with their clients emotionally.
2. They rely too much on one-way PowerPoint® slideshows, and are not diagnostic in their presentations.

3. They have no clear system for preparing, improving and perfecting their business presentations.

Since 1997, I've been selling complex products and services in business-to-business environments, helping corporations close six and seven figure deals through the power of Parable Point Presentations. Over the years, through extensive scholarly inquiry and field sales experience I have developed a unique, result-oriented, measurable system that is built around the ancient art and scientifically verified practice of business storytelling.

The following seven steps will give you the basics for winning more clients through business presentations. To get the most out of this workbook section, use these steps to prepare for a specific upcoming client meeting.

STEP 1: WHERE ARE YOU TODAY?

In order to win more clients, you must begin by examining your own current beliefs and thought patterns regarding the business presentation medium itself. What you think affects what you do, which in turn determines your results. Here are some things to consider before you deliver a presentation:

- A business presentation should never be exclusively about YOU. This is your chance to interact and share stories with your clients about THEIR challenges.
- Dynamic public speaking in business presentations is not a prerequisite to winning more clients.
- Your paradigms – the way you see the world – are at the center of how influential your business presentations are.

To get your mindset correctly aligned to achieve a successful presentation, answer the following questions about your current presentation mindset:

Where Are You Today?
Write down (honestly) where you are today on the Business Presentation

Continuum™. Are you a bullet-point, benefit-point or a parable-point presenter?

How Much Time Do You Spend Preparing for Meetings?
An hour? A day? A Week? What do you do to get prepared?

Dynamism vs. Magnetism
Do you fear public speaking? Do you find yourself relying too much on PowerPoint® or written bullet-points in your presentations? Do you believe that you have to be an eloquent speaker to be persuasive?

Facts Tell, but Stories Sell
Do you like to rely on facts to make your points? Do you like telling stories? Do you like listening to your clients' stories? What kind of stories do you tell?

Asking Questions
During business presentations, what is your ratio of talking versus asking questions? 70:30? 50:50? 40:60?

Logic vs. Emotion
Do you rely heavily on logic to make your points? Do you have specific strategies for moving your listeners emotionally?

Getting Ready For Your Presentation
In order to get ready for your business presentation, focus exclusively on learning, researching, and thinking about your client's needs. Literally step into their shoes so that all your stories, questions and issues are geared toward their needs: Write down the following:

- Prospective Client/Business Description:
- Industry/Company research:
- What Major Challenges are they experiencing?
- How does your product or service solve their major challenge?

Write down one PARABLE (a short story) that can be used to explain how your product or service solves their major challenge.

STEP 2: THE CLIENT'S BRAINPATH™

Influencing clients in a business presentation is all about moving them to a state of deep insight called 'Aha!' This is where the value perception gap between your product and their needs is closed. Achieving this state in the client's mind involves a process of mapping stories and parables to the brain's natural path of least resistance. This process, also known as 'traveling the BrainPath', is when you use parable points to communicate to people's emotional and logical brains. By following the BrainPath, you will establish trust, encourage participation, and deliver the feeling of 'Aha!'

Assuming you have a one-hour meeting, use the BrainPath™ template in Figure 12.1 to create a presentation storyboard and arrange your parables and points into three major areas. (Don't start with PowerPoint®! Multimedia is a second step after you create the storyboard).

Trust (Introduction: 5 minutes – Reptilian Brain)
What strategies and parables will you use to establish trust and credibility in your business presentation? What is your parable of WHO you are?

What is your parable of WHY they should listen to you? What is the client-focused purpose, process, and payoff for today's meeting?

Participation (Body: 45 minutes – Limbic Brain)
What customer challenges will you address today? What specific strategies and parables will you use to explain each challenge? What proof points and examples do you have for each parable? HOW will you encourage your listeners to participate with you so that this is not a one-way presentation?

'Aha!' (End: 5 minutes – Cortex Brain)
What deep insight, or 'Aha!' feeling will you deliver at the end of this presentation? What parable will you use to drive home your 'Aha?' What are the desired outcomes, next steps, and calls to action for this meeting?

Feedback
Reserve 5 minutes at the end for getting verbal audience or written ConversionTrack feedback. Here are some potential questions:

1. Was the presentation helpful in clarifying our business fit?

2. Did I credibly address your business challenges and needs?

3. Did you feel like you participated?

4. What were the three most important things you learned?

5. Did you experience an 'Aha!' – If so, in what area?

6. How will you use what you gained in this presentation?

7. Will you explain what you learned to others?

8. Would you like to learn more? Shall I contact you by email?

9. How can I improve this presentation?

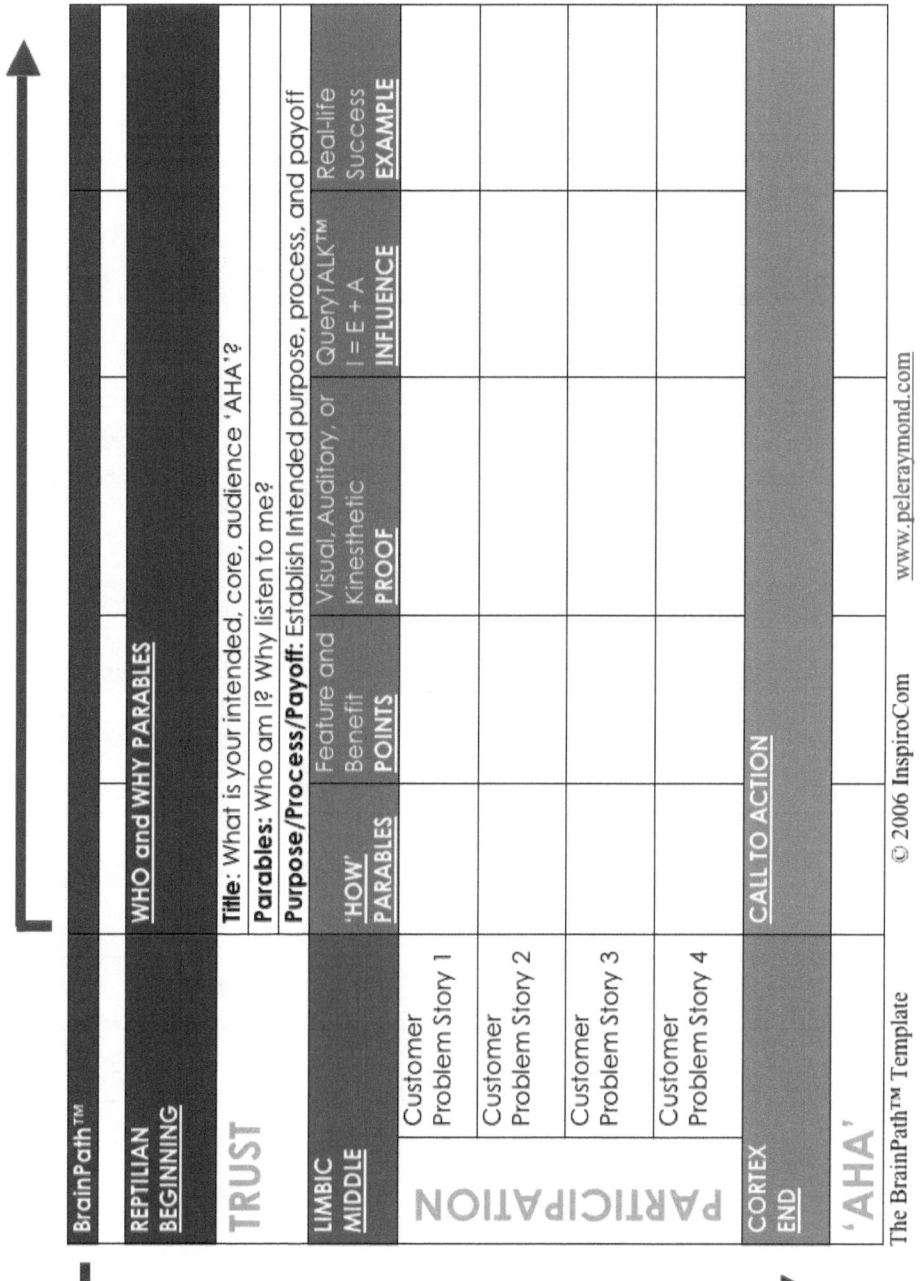

Figure 12.1. The BrainPath Storyboard Template

STEP 3: QUERYT.A.L.K.™

Now that you have designed the overall flow of your presentation, you need to focus on how you will deliver it. QueryT.A.L.K.™ is the process of speaking through questions that continuously encourage your clients to tell you their stories and become an integral part of the communication process. The acronym 'T.A.L.K.' encourages you to '**Touch** your audience emotionally, while involving them experientially through **Action, Laughter,** and **Knowledge.**'

Query
Remember – The best business presentations are 100% about the client. What specific questions will you ask your listeners in order to make sure they are sharing their stories and challenges during your presentation, and that your discussion is interactive and diagnostic?

List your Top Ten 'QueryTALK' Questions:

1. _____

2. _____

3. _____

4. _____

5. _____

6. _____

7. _____

8. _____

9. _____

10. _____

T. (Touch)
How will you touch your audience emotionally? What parables will you use?

A. (Action)
What will you ask your audience to do physically during the presentation? How will they participate? How will you use your own body language to convey certain points?

L. (Laughter)
What specific humor, jokes, or stories will you use to lighten up your audience?

K. (Knowledge)
What profound knowledge and insights will you impart on this audience that is emotionally meaningful to them?

Use the QueryTalk template in Figure 12.2 to fill in your content.

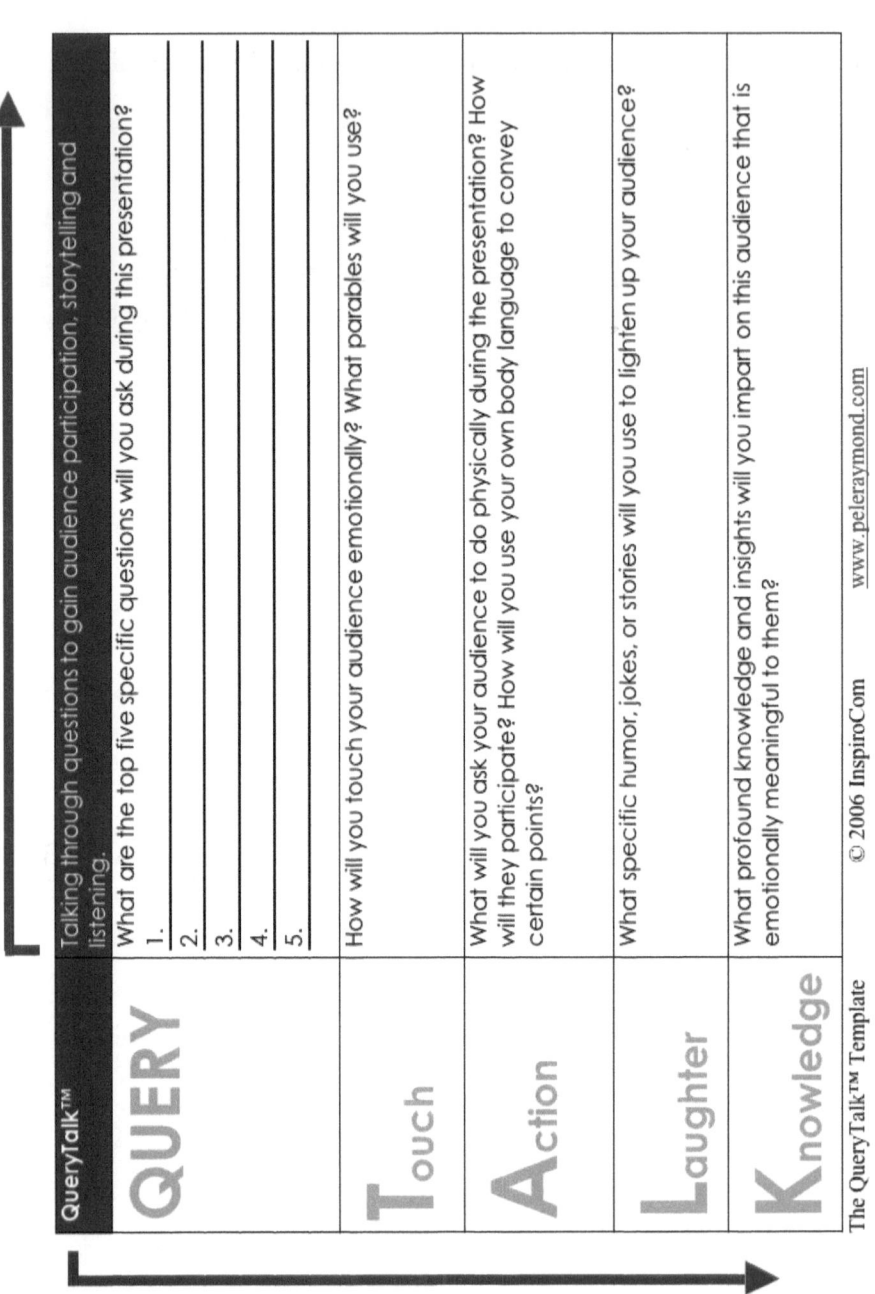

QueryTalk™	Talking through questions to gain audience participation, storytelling and listening.
QUERY	What are the top five specific questions will you ask during this presentation? 1. _____ 2. _____ 3. _____ 4. _____ 5. _____
Touch	How will you touch your audience emotionally? What parables will you use?
Action	What will you ask your audience to do physically during the presentation? How will they participate? How will you use your own body language to convey certain points?
Laughter	What specific humor, jokes, or stories will you use to lighten up your audience?
Knowledge	What profound knowledge and insights will you impart on this audience that is emotionally meaningful to them?

The QueryTalk™ Template   © 2006 InspiroCom   www.peleraymond.com

Figure 12.2. The QueryTalk™ Template For Delivering Presentations

STEP 4: YOUR PARABLE OF WHO

Now that you have structured your presentation and added your QueryTalk content, you need to construct the parables that you will use to make your points throughout the meeting.

The first thing you must establish in a business presentation is who you are and why your audience should listen to you – (i.e. Trust). Credibility and trust are the first things on the minds of your listeners. Instead of bullet-points that tersely state that you are the manager of this or that company, tell your audience a well-packaged, interesting story about yourself that doubles up as a way of preparing them for the influential, benefit-laden discussion you are about to lead them through.

In the first few minutes of your presentation, make sure that your parable describes WHO you are, and why they should listen to you.

What will be the main business point of your parable of WHO?

The Four 'C's of your Parable

1. What is the context of your story?

2. What is the conflict event in your story?

3. What is the change event in your story?

4. What is the conclusion of your story?

STEP 5: YOUR PARABLE OF WHY

Telling your clients who you are is very important, but equally important is that you establish early on why they should listen to you. You may have made that point somewhere in your parable of who, but you may not have fully answered one of their most burning questions:

Why are you any different from anyone else?

The answer to that question is your unique competitive advantage. Create a parable of WHY your clients should listen to you and not your competitors. Make sure that you address the following questions:

What is your unique approach to solving the client's challenge?

What specific testimonials do you have from other satisfied clients?

Do you have a guarantee of some kind that will reduce the client's risk?

Any other reasons "WHY YOU?"

STEP 6: YOUR PARABLE OF HOW

Throughout your business presentations, you will need to provide examples and proof of the points you are making. Once again, just telling people that your solution can do this or that is never as powerful as showing them how it actually did it through a story. As the popular saying goes, 'the proof is in the pudding'. If you are able to create and deliver short stories that show examples and proof of your features and benefits, you will go a long way in persuading listeners to see your point of view.

Start from the client's challenges

Go back to your list of client challenges, or use new ones presented during the meeting so far. For each challenge, address the following:

How does your solution address each customer challenge?

What parable of HOW your solution works can you use to explain this?

What is your proof that your solution will work for this client's challenges?

Can you give an example of satisfied clients - where your solution works today?

STEP 7: CONVERSIONTRACK™

In all other sales, marketing, or management activities, most practitioners use key performance indicators to track their progress - except in presentations! Most presenters have no idea what their presentation win-rates are, because they rarely get feedback or test and measure their results. In order to improve your client presentation conversion rates, you have to start by knowing what they are.

Do You Test and Measure Your Presentations?
Here are some questions to get you started in the process of testing and measuring your business presentations.

- What is your current presentation conversion rate for each phase of your selling process? 20%? 40%? 60%? Not sure?

- How many presentations do you typically give per month to prospects?

- How many prospects become clients or are moved closer to a sale as a result of those presentations?

- What feedback do clients give you regarding your presentations? How do you collect it?

- How would clients rate you in terms of Trust?

- How would clients rate you in terms of Participation?

- How would clients rate you in terms of delivering Ahas?

- Do you record your presentations for later (audio) review and analysis?

FINAL THOUGHTS

Congratulations! You have completed the journey! I want to thank you sincerely for accompanying me on this journey. I am confident that what you have learned here can positively impact your entire mindset, practices, and results when it comes to business presentations.

You have taken a bold look at your own paradigms and unspoken purpose for presentations, and you have challenged them and come out with a more 'customer-focused' mindset. Never again will you allow yourself to slip into the very human habit of communicating from a 'ME' paradigm.

You have also taken a hard look at the current myths about business presentations, including the ones that associate the fear of public speaking with the process of presenting value propositions to prospective clients. You are now fully aware that storytelling – which you have been doing all your life – is a much more powerful and influential way of winning clients than standard, (boring) bullet-point presentations.

You have immersed yourself into the biology of influence, the science of inspirational storytelling, and the power of parables as a vehicle for making points. Finally, you have learned the parable point presentation™ system, which is based on the three paradigm-busting philosophies of BrainPath™, QueryTalk™, and ConversionTrack™.

Remember these three core tenets of the **Parable Point Presentation™** system:

BrainPath™: It's not about you, the presenter. The true measure of presentation success is not based on what you do, but rather, it is based on your audience's actions and conversion rates. As a result, instead of teaching you mere presentation tactics, we empower you with a holistic process of thinking like your audience, so that you can more easily create and deliver messages that will connect with them.

QueryTalk™: Clients have been bored silly with the popular bullet-point, one-way presentation style that prevails in the corporate world today. Without an interactive, diagnostic presentation experience, prospective clients will tune you out. If you want to influence clients in presentations, you have to make parable points, and listen to their stories as well.

ConversionTrack™: In all other sales, marketing, or management activities, most practitioners use key performance indicators to track their progress as a strategy or improving performance - except in presentations! Most presenters have no idea what their presentation win-rates are, because they rarely practice, get feedback, or test and measure their results. In order to improve your client presentation conversion rates, you need a system for practicing, testing, and measuring your performance.

Our journey together is far from over; in fact, it has just begun. Feel free to request a keynote speech or a complimentary evaluation of your current go-to-market presentations. We at LeaderPractice will be happy to visit with you and your team, ask comprehensive questions about your business, and then help you clarify and diagnose what your presentation needs might be. If we mutually determine a business fit, we will work with you to select the appropriate process, (Parable Point Presentation workshops, training seminars, or coaching), that would most optimally meet your needs.

To your business presentation *success*!

Pelè Raymond Ugboajah, PhD
LeaderPractice
www.LeaderPractice.com
Helping B2B professionals win more clients in the complex sale.

ABOUT THE AUTHOR

Pelè Raymond Ugboajah, PhD, is a trainer, coach, and award-winning speaker on the subjects of leadership, presentation skills and winning more clients in the complex sale. Early in his career, Pelè was one of PTC's first Windchill 'evangelists', helping to turn its flagship product from a middleware toolkit to a $200-million-dollar-a-year business in just two years. Later, as director of marketing at EDS, he led the business presentation effort to establish the $20-billion-dollar corporation as a global leader in the enterprise software marketplace.

With over 10 years in entrepreneurship, corporate B2B sales and marketing, Pelè has helped organizations and professionals win more clients through business presentation workshops, training seminars, and corporate consulting. He is the author of "PARABLE POINT PRESENTATIONS: The Most Effective System For Winning More Clients In The Complex Sale." He holds BA and B.Arch. degrees from the University of Minnesota, an MBA from American Intercontinental University, and a PhD in Business (Organization & Management/Leadership) from Capella University.

To request Pelè for keynote speaking, consulting, or training, please visit www.leaderpractice.com

REFERENCES

Aristotle (350 BC). *Rhetoric, translated by W. Rhys Roberts.* Whitefish, MT: Kessinger Publishing.

Armstrong, D. (1992). *Managing by storying around: A new method of leadership.* New York: Bantam Double Day Dell.

Atkinson, C. (2005). *Beyond bullet-points: Using Microsoft PowerPoint® to create presentations that inform, motivate, and inspire.* Redmond, WA: Microsoft Press.

Barsade, S. G. (2002). The ripple effect: Emotional contagion and its influence on group behavior. *Administrativee Science Quarterly, 47*(4), 644-675.

Bass, B. M. (1990). From transactional to transformational leadership: Learning to share the vision. *Organizational Dynamics, 18*(3), 19-21.

Beckwith, H. (1997). *Selling the invisible: A field guide to modern marketing.* New York: Warner Books.

Brown, L. (2004). *Live Your Dreams.* Presentation delivered at the 2004 Better Life Media Leadership Seminar. Minneapolis, MN.

Burns, J. M. (1979). *Leadership.* New York: Harper Row.

Cialdini, R. B. (2001). Harnessing the power of persuasion. *Harvard Business Review, 79*(9), 72-79.

Clarke, B., & Crossland, R. (2002). *Leader's voice: How communication can inspire action and get results.* New York: Select Books.

Claxton, G. (2004). Learning is learnable, (and we ought to teach it). In Sir John Cassell (Ed.), *Ten years on: National commission for education report.* Bristol, UK: National Commission for Education.

Crick, F. (1994). *Astonishing hypothesis: the scientific search for the soul.* New York: Touchstone.

Curry, J. L. (2004). *Mysteries of the kingdom: the literary path to wisdom.* Roanoke, TX: See Again Press.

Damasio, A. (2001). Fundamental Feelings. *Nature, 413*(6858), 781.

Darwin, C. (1872). *Expression of the emotions in man and animals.* New York: W. W. Norton & Company.

Dorsey, D. A. (1999). *Literary structure of the old testament: A commentary on Genesis-Malachi* (2nd ed.). Grand Rapids, MI: Baker Academic.

Edmunds, S. W. (1979). Differing perceptions of small business problems. *American Journal of Small Business, 3*(4), 1-14.

Ekman, P. (1992). Are there basic emotions? *Psychological Review, 99*(3), 550-553.

Friedlander, S. (1992). *When you hear hoofbeats think of a zebra.* Costa Mesa, CA: Mazda Publishers.

Gardner, H., & Laskin, E. (1995). *Leading minds: An anatomy of leadership.* New York: Basic Books.

Gazzaniga, M. S. (1998). The split brain revisited. *Scientific American, 279*(1), .

Gerber, M. (1995). *E-Myth revisited: Why most small businesses don't work, and what to do about it.* New York: Harper Business.

Gladwell, M. (2002). *Tipping point: How little things can make a big difference.* New York: Brown and Company.

Goleman, D. (1992). Introduction by Daniel Goleman. In S. Friedlander (Ed.), *When you hear hoofbeats think of a zebra* (p. viii). Costa Mesa, CA: Mazda Publishers.

Goleman, D. (2006). *Social intelligence: the new science of human relationships.* New York: Bantam Dell.

Goleman, D., Boyatzis, R., & McKee, A. (2002). Primal leadership: Realizing the power of emotional intelligence. *Personnel Psychology, 55*(4), 1030-1033.

Goodman, A. (2004). *Storytelling as best practice: How stories strengthen your organization, engage your audience, and advance your mission* (2nd ed.). Los Angeles, CA: A Goodman.

Goodman, A. (2005). Think you're a good presenter? Your audience may disagree. In Andy Goodman (Ed.), *Free Range Thinking* (p.). Los Angeles, CA: A Goodman.

Hawkins, D. R. (1995). *Power vs. force: the hidden determinants of human behavior.* Sedona, AZ: Veritas Publishing.

Headd, B. (2003). Redefining business success: Distinguishing between closure and failure. *Small Business Economics, 21,* 51-61.

Hopkins, C. C. (1923). *Scientific Advertising.* Chicago, IL: NTC Business Books.

Jung-Beeman, M., et al. (2004). Neural activity when people solve problems with insight. *PLoS Biology, 2*(4), 500-510.

Kahan, S. (2006). The power of storytelling to jumpstart collaboration. *Journal for Quality & Participation, 29*(1), 23-25.

Knight, S. (2005). *NLP at work: the difference that makes a difference in business* (2nd ed.). Finland: WS Bookwell.

Kuhn, T. S. (1996). *Structure of scientific revolutions* (3rd ed.). Chicago: The University of Chicago Press.

LeDoux, J. E. (1995). Emotion: Clues from the brain. *Annual Review of Psychology, 46*(1), 209-235.

Ledoux, J. E. (1998). *Emotional brain: the mysterious underpinnings of emotional life.* New York: Touchstone.

Martin, J., & Powers, M. (1979, September). *If case examples provide no proof, why under-utilize statistical information?* Paper presented at the meeting of the American Psychological Association. .

Mayer, R. E. (2001). *Multimedia learning.* Cambridge, UK: Cambridge University Press.

Mayer, R. E. (2002). Rote versus meaningful learning. *Theory Into Practice, 41*(4), para 2.

Mayer, R., & Moreno, R. (). *A Learner-Centered Approach to Multimedia Explanations: Deriving Instructional Design Principles from Cognitive Theory.* Retrieved January 9, 2007, from http://imej.wfu.edu/articles/2000/2/05/index.asp

McConkie, M. L., & Boss, R. W. (1994). Using stories as an aid to consultation. *Public Administration Quarterly, 17*(4), 377-395.

McQuarrie, E. F., & Phillips, B. J. (2005). Indirect persuasion in advertising. *Journal of Advertising, 34*(2), 7-20.

McQuarrie, E. F., & Phillips, B. J. (). , , .

Mehrabian, A. (1972). *Non-verbal communication.* New York: Walter De Gruyter Inc.

Metcalfe, J., Funnell, M., & Gazzaniga, M. S. (1995). Right hemisphere memory superiority: Studies of a split-brain patient. *Psychological Science, 6*(3), 157-164.

Microsoft. (2006). *Killer Presentations – wake up your audience!* Retrieved October 25, 2006, from Microsoft Web Site: http://www.microsoft.com/uk/atwork/office/killerpresentation s.mspx

Moncrief, W. C., & Shipp, S. H. (1997). *Sales management: Strategy, technology, skills* (2nd ed.). Boston, MA: Pearson Customer Publishing.

Paul, R. W. (1984). The Socratic spirit: An answer to Louis Goldman. *Education Leadership, XLII,* 63-64.

Phoel, C. M. (2006). Leading words: How to use stories to change minds and ignite action. *Harvard Management Communication Letter, 3*(2), 3-5.

Satterfield, M. (2006). *Gentle Rain Marketing.* Retrieved November 30, 2006, from Gentle Rain Marketing Web Site: http://www.gentlerainmarketing.com/product_stories.html

Sewell, C., & Brown, P. B. (1990). *Customers for life: How to turn that one-time buyer into a lifetime customer.* New York: Simon and Schuster.

Steil, L. K. (2006). *You got questions? So do I!* Paper presented at the meeting of the NSA-MN Fireside Forum. Minneapolis, MN.

Weinreich, B. (1988). *Yiddish Folktales* (1st ed.). New York: Pantheon Books.

Wyer, R. S., & Collins, J. E. (1992). A theory of humor elicitation. *Psychological Review, 99*(4), 663-688.